Careers by Design

A Headhunter's Secrets
for Success and Survival
in Graphic Design

by Roz Goldfarb

Revised Edition

Allworth Press
New York

Published by Allworth Press
An imprint of Allworth Communications
10 East 23rd Street, New York, NY 10010

Cover design by Michael Bierut, Pentagram Design, New York, NY

Book design by Charlie Sharp, Sharp Des!gns, Holt, MI

ISBN: 1-880559-57-9

Library of Congress Catalog Card Number: 96-84633

Careers by Design

Contents

Introduction

All my colleagues agree. The business is changed; it's different. Casual conversations over lunch or chance meetings on the street all focus on this point. "What's new?" one asks. "Everything. The business surely is different . . . is just not the same," is the answer, said sometimes wistfully, sometimes in frustration. It's been nearly five years since I originally wrote this book and graphic design without question has changed, driven by technology and changing markets. These changes have driven the need to update and, naturally, it is the passages devoted to those subjects that reflect the significant revisions.

There is another change, less obvious to the public but clear to anyone who needs to hire staff. It is a syndrome that no one can quite explain. Throughout the country there are more jobs available than there are qualified people. This is in spite of an amazing number of people entering the design business. Larry Keeley, president of The Doblin Group, the Chicago-based strategic design planning firm, spoke at the International Design Conference in Aspen in 1995. He gave the following chilling statistics: "In the United States, according to the best available estimates—and it's very hard to get a good idea—there are between 400 and 600 four-year graphic design schools. There are certainly over 600 schools that issue design degrees of one type or another. These folks, in the U.S. alone, produce an estimated 50 thousand graduates annually . . . The same phenomenon [is] going on in Europe . . . [where] 180 thousand students are studying design full time . . . The Japanese . . . [are] producing the same abundance of supply of designers that we're seeing elsewhere in the world. . . . So the critical question is, can the industry begin to absorb all this incoming talent?"

So, what is the problem? With all these aspiring designers, why are positions unfilled? Is it the educational system or just elements of natural selection, the survival of the fittest, the requirements of traveling up the "food chain" that creates this disparity? Clearly the operative word must be "talent." While the definitions may be highly subjective, there are standards of business sophistication and aesthetic savvy that are necessary to a successful career. Hopefully this book will help designers learn that while it may be the first requirement, talent alone is not enough.

While change may be a constant, work-related criteria have not changed at all. The need for excellence and creativity in the workplace, be it in design or in business strategy, never changes. A strong work ethic combined with sensitivity to human values are always a necessary commitment. The need to focus on life-style and family needs remains and will always remain. My lesson, one more time, is that while everything seems new and different, the core values never change.

Life is a series of choices. To my mind, choice is the key to the game of life. Being able to make informed choices means having freedom. It means having the freedom to choose and direct the course of your future, the freedom to change directions, and the freedom to feel in control of your actions. This kind of freedom does not come easily. It requires a commitment to work, research, and to yourself. Truthfully, I also think it requires a certain amount of luck. But if you are worldly and aware, it is amazing how luck can find you. There are people who make their opportunities happen and those who wouldn't recognize an opportunity if it stared them in the face.

The information required to function with "freedom of choice" falls into three categories.

■ You must have the proper education—exposure to the

concepts and tools necessary for your personal development.

- You must have the ambition and commitment to want to do your personal best.
- You must be knowledgeable and informed about your chosen career and the world at large.

After a twenty-five–year career in design placement and design education, I'm continually amazed to learn what little information exists on the hard-core issues of the design business. The concept of design as a business is the focus of this book, for that is what it is—a business. To achieve a design career, you will require an understanding of the structure of business and how the various components of design interrelate with each other and to graphic design as a whole. It's the ability to see the forest and be able to discern different species of trees. This is the kind of information that would enable students, professionals, career counselors, and educators to make important life choices. For some people, these initial choices, made early in life, often determine unalterable courses. I often refer to my "Smorgasbord Theory of Choice" when lecturing to students. The theorem goes like this: Pretend you're at a wedding reception where you are presented with a very long smorgasbord. You are only allowed one plate. You therefore get in line, take a plate, and start to fill it with wonderful, delicious food. The only problem is, as your plate fills up, you realize you haven't reached the end of the table. As you approach the end, you see the selection is better and you'd prefer that food—but, you have no more room on your dish! Had you only known! You now realize it would have been wiser to have scanned the length of the table before getting in line. Although life does not allow us to scan the length of our table before getting in line, there are some things we can control through knowledge. Choosing a career or making a career change at least affords us an educated guess and, with the information in this book, a much broader concept of what awaits.

Too often I have interviewed people well on in their careers who have only a vague notion of which paths their careers might travel. Early on they were propelled by only an intuitive recognition that they were talented and lacked any real sense of the field they wished to enter. Artistic talent usually surfaces very early in life. Most creative people first recognize that part of their personality when they are young children and in later years acknowledge a need to find a practical application of their abilities. When that interest turns to design it is a rare person who has an informed, realistic picture of what graphic design is about, how it relates to advertising, and where in the scheme of things he fits in—for most people it's totally unclear.

Ideally, if career information is needed, high school students and their parents will seek out help from guidance counselors and art teachers. Unfortunately, these individuals rarely have the necessary information either. Their own education and life experience have not given them enough exposure. While I was the director of the Pratt Phoenix School of Design (a division of Pratt Institute) in the late 1970s, I ran a continuing education program for the New York City Board of Education's high school teachers. These short seminars were designed to offer an overview of the different areas of design, the opportunities available, the basic job descriptions, and salary ranges available. It proved to be an eye-opener, for many of these teachers were either guidance counselors or art teachers who never had contact with such direct and pragmatic information. It should be noted that, in most cases, accurate data is available from the admissions offices of art colleges that specialize in professional programs. There are a number of professional design colleges in this county (see Index), but it should be indicated that most of them have a specific educational point of view and specialization within their curricula. (See chapter 14.)

It is important for the readers of this book to know how and why my opinions were formed. After nearly ten years as an administrator and educator at Pratt Institute, I joined an executive recruitment firm specializing in placing designers and art directors in jobs within the design and advertising fields. While at Pratt I became aware of the urgent need for proper career information—something I never had. At that time my efforts were directed toward developing courses, workshops, and seminars for high school and college level students and teachers. As a recruiter, and now as president of my own firm, Roz Goldfarb Associates, I'm subjected daily to the vicissitudes of hiring criteria and firing practices, to the demands employers place on their staff, and to the frustrations people experience in the workplace on both sides of the fence. I have been given the unique opportunity of observing careers in the making, as well as careers that flounder. I see these occurrences from a very special vantage point, for we are the consultants whose very existence depends on our ability to keep a confidence. Our clients range from the design gurus—the movers and shakers whose fame precedes them, to small entrepreneurs and all others who recognize that their business' success depends on the quality of their creative personnel. Both our clients (those who pay our fees to find them the "perfect person") and our candidates (those who wish another career opportunity and position) confide their motivations to us, knowing that information is necessary for us to function accurately and knowing it will be kept in confidence. The vast number of negotiations; the hard decisions and profound, fundamental choices we experience in the daily drama of our office by far outstrip the designer or art director who has probably (and hopefully) changed jobs less than ten times in a lifetime. In this book, I will draw upon these experiences through case histories or anecdotes; but, of course, names will never be divulged.

In providing any overview of design, clear distinctions must be made between design and advertising. The types of jobs that will lead to realistic careers must be discussed, as well as what one can expect to earn in these positions, and what kind of a lifestyle that may dictate. With proper information, and more than a little good luck, an informed decision for a life choice or career change is possible. I hope we can provide a guide to entering a fascinating world and to some of its opportunities. As I've mentioned, you can't make a decision if you don't know what the choices are. Too often we're asked to do just that! Often at Pratt, I would encounter an irate parent, who strongly believed that the investment of time and money into an art education was impractical and wasteful. I'll never forget the student applying to Pratt Institute who tearfully told me why he couldn't accept our offer of admission and partial scholarship. His father, a teacher, would have gladly paid for his education if he were to become an accountant or the like, but would never contribute his hard-earned money to further a design education. Nor would the father allow me the opportunity to explain that one could earn a respectful and sometimes highly compensated income in design and that his son could achieve the personal gratification necessary for a complete life.

The graphic designer holds a unique position in our

expanding world of communications. While the design business has grown and matured substantially in the United States, there is still little public recognition of its impact on our everyday existence. Simply put, everything we wear, touch, read, ride in, and live in has been created by a designer. Our newspapers, magazines, and books; our household appliances and automobiles; the packages that cover every object imaginable and entice us to buy; the graphic images, logotypes, and signs in stores and restaurants, as well as their identity, menus, and, sometimes, even their names; the amusement parks we take our children to; the famous cartoon characters we become attached to, and the licensed products we buy with their logos or images; the shapes of cosmetic jars, bottles, compacts, lipsticks, and their packaging; the gift wrap and cards for presents; the incalculable numbers of brochures, annual reports, and corporate literature—all have been developed or designed by graphic and industrial designers. The list is endless.

And most important, design is a business. It is not enough to want to create something that is beautiful. Design awards and professional recognition are tremendous incentives. Sometimes a design will even enter the collection of a famous museum. But design must also reflect a responsiveness to market factors, and designers must be knowledgeable about sociological and economic trends. Today we all are well aware of being members of a global economic community. The design community, as part of the business community, has played an integral part in these developments. Many firms have an international reach through either branch offices or a multinational client base. Anyone entering these fields must recognize the need to participate in the core of the business to be in a position to make the important decisions. All these factors contribute to the ability to make career and life choices.

This book's goal is to identify the distinctions between various areas of specialization, to analyze the talent and personality most apt to thrive, to point to the newer, developing areas where increased opportunity may lie, and to give an approximation of the salary levels currently prevalent in these fields. Generalizations are always dangerous, but this book will try to discern the characteristics of major market segments, as well as look to the future.

In defining graphic design, I have included a discussion of

industrial design only in its relationship to graphic design. I have eliminated the associated fields of photography and illustration. Both are formidable creative areas practiced by many designers. However, while graphic designers may utilize photography and illustration in their own work, or art direct photographers and illustrators, the converse is rarely true. Photographers and illustrators are rarely graphic designers. The exceptional people who do it all are legendary. This book is geared to the student, the young professional, the established professional seeking change, and to the art educator. It is written from a point of view acquired through years of dealing with everyday, real life experience, and designed to inform in a concise manner.

I especially want to express my personal thanks and gratitude to Rita Armstrong, Jessica Goldfarb, and all those who have contributed to the chapter on digital design: Red Burns, Steve Dolbow, Bruce Wands, Tom Weisz, and Kenneth Cooke. Clearly, it is the technological advances in this business that have produced the greatest change. Interactive media is moving so fast that it's difficult to keep perspective and have a viewpoint, but these people have been generous in offering their insights. Rita Armstrong and Jessica Goldfarb are associates of Roz Goldfarb Associates. Rita Armstrong is the career counselor that everyone needs. She has provided the important, day-to-day information for job placement of computer designers. Jessica Goldfarb, partnering with Rita in Interactive Media, has quickly become a leading recruiter/ advisor, respected for her knowledgeable grasp of the business' nuances. I'm very lucky.

This revised edition also includes the thoughts of others who have taken time from their busy schedules to share their experiences. Thanks to Clement Mok, Louis Nelson, and Nancye Green.

Ultimately, we are the sum of our experiences. My professional life has been enriched continually through the fellowship of many very talented and sometimes brilliant people of vastly divergent view points. This diversity in itself has educated me, for I have always been fascinated by their life experiences and business philosophies. By keeping an open mind, listening intently, evaluating, accepting, and rejecting view points, I have formulated many of my own opinions. It would be negligent for me not to mention a few of these individuals. In 1992 I thanked a wonderful group of people.

I'd like to revise that list if only to add some new friends. In New York: Clive Chajet, Barry Green, and Jerry Kuyper of Lippincott & Margulies; all the folks—past and present—at Siegel & Gale, Alan Siegel, Don Ervin, Kenneth Cooke, Steve Dolbow, and Scott Lerman; Steff Geisbuhler, a principal of Chermayeff & Geismar; Richard Saul Wurman; Richard Brandt of Landor Claude Salzberger at Diefenbach Elkins; . Elsewhere: Andrew Swift, my colleague in London; Jelle van der Toorn Vrijthoff of Total Design in Amsterdam; in Los Angeles, Saul Bass and Gerry Rosentzweig, both of whom have died within the last year; the educators at Art Center College of Design; Henry Steiner in Hong Kong; the thousands of people all over the country whom I have interviewed and who generously shared their perceptions, dreams, and frustrations; and, not least, the staff and faculty of Pratt Institute in Brooklyn who enabled me, as a member of their team, to begin this journey into design.

And thanks are due to the associates of Roz Goldfarb Associates. They are Rita Armstrong, Penny Burrow, Donna Golba, Jessica Goldfarb, Marion Thunberg, and Connie Kail Wolf, all of whom have shared their knowledge and experience with me. A thank you is also due to Ann Conner, who has always been terrific help. We are, in addition to an integrated business unit, much like an extended family. I am surrounded by unique people and I'm in matchless company.

Finally there's my family, who, at the end of the day, are the most important focus of my world. My mother, who lived eighty-eight years, owned a dress factory in New York's very tough garment center before anyone ever thought of women's liberation. She set us all quite an example. My husband Ben, my partner and best friend; our three daughters Meryl, Leslie, and Jessica, who are making their own life's choices and our grandson, Matthew, our next generation—all are precious beyond description.

I'll close with a toast to all those not mentioned, who have given me the opportunity to learn and those who, no doubt, will be part of my future. All have allowed me to experience the fruit of my life's choices.

ROZ GOLDFARB
September 1996

1

What Is Graphic Design?

How many people can give a reasonable definition of graphic design? It's not a profession that has a clear identity in the mind of the general public. Design is a much used word, and can mean many things. Often when people refer to designers they may have a generalized notion of fashion design or engineering design, as well as automotive, product, and architectural design, and perhaps industrial design. But usually graphic design is grouped with that ubiquitous term "advertising." Advertising is, after all, well known. We have seen it in film and fiction. It's all-pervasive in our society, but it's not design. Tell someone at a party you're a graphic designer and you'll probably find they will consider you part of the advertising world or confuse your job with graphic reproduction and the printing industries. Or, worse, somebody may say, "Oh, I understand, you're a commercial artist," which is a totally archaic term. The public believes it knows what architecture, interior design, or advertising is about, but the identifier graphic design can be a mystery. It's interesting to note the amount of confusion among educators and other professionals as well. Few can identify the difference between an industrial designer, environmental designer, or graphic designer.

The Designer's Role in Society and Business

While design has not traditionally been one of the glamour professions, fame may soon be awaiting the anonymous designer. With the advent of the 1990s, design has become a hot media topic. Business publications are beginning to focus on the correlation between design and the success of product launches. The *Wall Street Journal* now has a column entitled, "Form and Function," although it is mostly devoted to industrial design. Every year *Business Week* offers a cover story on industrial design. In their special issue of August 23, 1990, themed "Innovation: The Global Race," the editors predicted: "Design is to the '90s what finance was to the '80s, and marketing to the '70s: It is the corporate buzzword for the new decade." Unfortunately, as I write this in 1996 this perception is not yet the rule, although various professional organizations have tried to promote the importance of design to the business community and there have been discussions about the value of licensing graphic designers as a method of influencing public recognition.

The effect of good, functional design in the marketplace has long been recognized in other parts of the world. We all are aware of the impact of German, Italian, and Japanese design in product and the automotive field; Italian design in lighting; French or Italian in fashion; and Scandinavian design in silver. It's a sad commentary about our society to realize that it's only recently that corporate America is at last recognizing that good design can sell. This recognition will shed new light on the profession of design and advance the perception of the graphic designer's contribution to the "bottom line." Graduate schools are slowly incorporating a recognition of design's interaction with product development. The London Business School has been on the leading edge of this move in education. The Design Management Institute, as well as the newer Corporate Design Foundation, seek to promote the relationship between effective design and the successful corporation.

However, while the graphic designer's role today may not yet be readily identifiable to the average individual as it is to the sophisticated corporation, the designer does have an

Designers as Arbiters of Taste enormous impact on our society. Designers create the look and feel of our world. They are the *arbiters* of taste and lead the way to how we perceive what's good, tasteful, stylish—or not, as the case may be. As pointed out in my foreword, virtually everything around us is created through design. The diversity and global reach of the designer's influence is so vast it can be difficult to comprehend. It certainly must not be overlooked or undervalued. Designers create and interpret sociological trends. They create the mood and shape of our world. Designers, therefore, *must be worldly* in the true sense of the word. They must be aware of all things that affect change and style. Politics and finance, entertainment and literature, fine arts and history, food and music—all play important roles in our constantly transforming environment. In other words, they must observe and perhaps partake in all facets of life. No one entering this field should be content with a confining definition of creativity. Creativity is not just the action of the imagination and a particular skill like drawing, writing, or composing. One must also have the ability to analyze, assimilate, and interpret the past and present structure of society in order to interpret the present and foretell the future.

As there is little in our daily experience that is not de-signed by designers, the graphic designer has an unusual opportunity to make a personal contribution to our world in this expanding business environment. As a designer you can derive creative fulfillment from your efforts and still earn a reasonable, and in some cases sizable, income from those efforts. The combination of personal and economic satisfaction offers many individuals a gratifying avenue for their talent. Graphic designers, by and large, may sometimes complain about long hours and low pay scale, but mostly they are a committed and satisfied group, because they can always see a tangible result of their work effort.

Design in Our Eaily Experience

And design is a field which is expanding. It's an exciting time to be in graphic design. Design firms are growing in their complexity and size. Like advertising, design is becoming an increasingly global business. Many of the products and services marketed by the clients of large design consultancies are done so on a global basis. Cross-cultural design and marketing is an increasingly important aspect of communications. Another aspect of globalization is the effect of industry wide mergers, joint ventures, and international expansion—all of which produce companies that are viable in the international arena.

While many firms have expanded through acquisition—

such as buying out another design firm in another city—in the past few years many design firms have been acquired by advertising agencies. There is a newly developed recognition in the profitability of "below the line" companies, as well as a desire to diversify the agencies' services within the communications fields. The term "below the line" refers to companies without media placement. Agencies traditionally derive income from a percentage mark-up of media placement—meaning a mark-up on the dollars spent for their clients in buying time and space in broadcast (television and radio) or in print publications. New media or interactive media are redefining all concepts of media placement.

Clearing Up Some Confusion about Advertising and Design

Advertising differs from design in many ways. Advertising is always a visual and written solution to a marketing strategy. The message is to sell a product or service. The key word here is "sell." Never underestimate that intent. Whether it's television, print advertisements found in newspapers and magazines, direct mail, or direct response ads, it is all there to send the message "buy me."

In most agencies the key players are the creative team, working in conjunction with the marketing account executives (jokingly known as the "suits"). The creative team is composed of art directors and copywriters, who work in tandem. This combined team of creative and marketing talent devises the advertising strategy with and for the client. Each offers a different area of expertise to form the final direction. The media department makes the necessary decisions for placement of the advertising in print and broadcast, because they buy the space and time. Nowadays, agencies are adding to this mix by developing or creating relationships with new media agencies. Advertising is a huge business whose budgets dwarf those allocated to the design field. And as we all know, advertising is a powerful force in our media intensive society, saturating us with concepts like "Solutions for a small planet" for IBM, or Nike's "Just do it!"

It is important to note that the business of advertising (as well as design) is ultimately its creative product. It is the art directors and the copywriters who "make" advertising. It is this creative output which makes advertising and the various design areas a unique business. And these are service businesses, another special characteristic. They are dependent upon the quality of their product and dependent on clients who "buy into" or believe in the power of the work as an effective business practice. Some advertising, especially direct marketing, can be tracked to be made accountable. Mostly, however, it is far more intangible—really a perception of success.

In any discussion of advertising and design, it should be noted that it is in sales promotion that the two disciplines meet. While sales promotion will be discussed at length in chapter 6, let it suffice to say now that the brochures, marketing tools, and point-of-sale products developed by the sales promotional divisions within advertising agencies need talent that can work with design values and marketing driven concepts. These promotion groups, at their best, offer designers opportunities to work on a variety of diversified assignments not always available in studio environments.

Therefore, the two immediate distinctions between advertising and design are that (1) design firms, while they may work in new media, by definition, do not place traditional media, and, (2) designers generally do not create print advertising and television campaigns. *When firms place media, they are considered, by definition, agencies.*

In recruiting talent for our clients, we find that the ability to work with copy is frequently a key ingredient in the job description. To work with copy means the designer must be able to visually interpret the copy concepts. Many graphic designers are more comfortable working strictly with graphic symbols and visual images without incorporating headline concepts or detailed copy.

Designers produce product and image-conscious sales tools for goods and services for multi-national firms all over the world. For example, companies such as Avon or Colgate produce products that are sold throughout the world. The designs of these products usually have to be altered for the marketing conditions of the geographical area, and, in some cases, that may mean changing the name as well. An annual report or corporate brochure may be produced in many languages; a retail chain will need its graphic imaging subtly defined for another culture.

Design's Impact on Style

As the importance of design receives ever-increasing acknowledgment from the media, its impact can also be seen in the emergence of specialty gift shops marketing "design savvy" products. Design departments in museums have been highlighting the important role of graphic and industrial design for years. The Museum of Modern Art in New York, for example, has had a seminal role in design appreciation and has now mastered the art of merchandising chosen products through its store and catalogues. All of this attention bodes well for the growing prestige of the designer. It is a direct response to the proven influence design has on business profitability and an affirmation that design has created the look and feel of our world. Design determines how we perceive what's good, tasteful, and stylish—or not— as the case may be. As noted earlier, corporate America is now recognizing what Europeans have known for a long time: That design is big business, and that it drives successful marketing. That good design sells. That a well-designed package, a good product design, can sell everything from cars to appliances. A well-designed retail image will move shoppers and merchandise. An excellent corporate identity program can affect the entire perception of the company, even on Wall Street.

The Business Issues of Design

So the bottom line is the bottom line! The importance of the graphic designer and graphic design as a profession is ultimately its impact on business. Therefore, although graphic design incorporates an aesthetic experience and a creative endeavor, it is its alliance to business, its ability to service clients' needs, that defines its place and status in today's economy. The art student pursuing a graphic design education must acknowledge design's role in the business community. Not to recognize this factor is an act of unnecessary idealism, resulting in a foolhardy conclusion. Without question the overriding common denominator of the most successful people in graphic design is their ability to maintain the highest creative standards without losing sight of their role as directors of a business.

I've often thought it a shame that fundamental business courses are not taught within the standard curriculum found in professional art colleges. Business insight is necessary to run your own business, to understand your clients' businesses, and to understand how to solve your clients' problems. If you are going to design an annual report, you'd better be able to understand what the financial data in the back of the book represents. If you're going to design a corporate identity program, you should know how that corporation functions in the marketplace, what you need to convey in terms of its image, and how that image will affect the company's internal structure, as well as its external communications. In short, you need to know how the business community operates. Much of the "phase 1" strategies and planning for design solutions are currently assigned to account executives and marketing planners within design firms. In fact, most large design firms define themselves as "Marketing Communications Consultants." While these roles will be discussed in chapter 3, I want to emphasize how important it is that the student or design professional does not remain in a naive vacuum, utilizing her creative instincts to make things look "pretty." The role of the professional graphic designer is to identify the client's communication problems and to find solutions that are aesthetically pleasing and communicate a proper message to the public; and to do so in a timely manner and on budget. Most hiring requests today emphasize the need for someone who is not only supremely talented, but also "smart"; someone who understands the business needs of the firm and can verbally, as well as visually, communicate them.

Is Design for You?

The individual determined to seek a career in the creative arts often seems to recognize this goal from a relatively early age. The ability to draw is always admired in children and praise often encourages the desire to become an "artist." Obviously, it's a long road from those origins to identifying graphic design as the chosen path. The roots, however, are important. But out of those roots must evolve a designer with a love of typography, color, and materials; with a desire to communicate through visual media. The designer must be a committed individual with a strong, determined desire to do good work. This book will point out the paths through the maze of choices within graphic design.

The designer must also become a sophisticated person, knowledgeable and articulate about politics, business, and all the arts—music, painting, history, food, and travel. The designer is a communicator. After all, how can one success-fully communicate to a society without being a full-fledged citizen of that society? To compound the issue, our society is now global, and therefore everything needed on a national basis is now a global issue.

These are the characteristics of a successful designer. The profession is stimulating in its vast breadth and exposure to every sector of the global business community. The indi-vidual who desires this direction must be prepared to enter this community with the knowledge and skills required to make a contribution.

Is graphic design for you? Only you can say for sure, but you can expose yourself though this book and other resources to reach an educated decision. If you have the motivation, go for it. Many people change careers during their adult life-time. Many do not end up doing what they thought they would. It is always fascinating to ask individuals you admire what they thought they would become. The answers are often surprising. ■

2

The Structure of Graphic Design

We have just examined the essential nature of graphic design and familiarized ourselves with the role of the designer in our society. It is now time to consider the nature of the creative product, how it services the marketing needs of business, and to discover the many parts which form the whole of graphic design. What may have seemed a simple classification is, in fact, an umbrella term for a sophisticated network of graphic-based communications disciplines. It is important to distinguish between these fields of endeavor for a clear understanding of the interrelationships within graphic design. A structural knowledge of the differing aspects of design is critical because, although these aspects interface with each other individually, they connect and correlate with the whole. In addition they characteristically define the role of the professional. This perspective needs to be seen with some historical context as well, for with the passage of time and the refinement of the business, these fragments of graphic design have often branched off to form areas of specialization.

Therefore, the perspective offered in this and the next chapters should help people realize their career goals, as well as more completely understand the essential nature of graphic design. And what are we talking about when we say graphic design? Classically we mean:

- Brand Identity (branding) and Packaging Design
- Corporate Identity—visual identifiers, logotype, and naming
- Corporate Communications and Corporate Literature—including information architecture, interactive media, corporate promotion, and annual reports
- Editorial Design
- Environmental Design—two- and three-dimensional design of a space, including exhibition design (also considered a part of Industrial Design)
- Retail Identity—similar to corporate identity, but applied to the retail sector
- Sales Promotion (can be an adjunct to advertising)

Ask most people participating in these fields to name their profession and they'll probably respond, graphic design, although there are many who now prefer information architecture. While that response is, of course, true, many designers find their day-to-day work focused on only a small segment of this complex field.

The Rise of Specialization

In order to discuss these areas of specialization, as they relate to the whole and as individual fields of endeavor, let us use an old, but appropriate, metaphor. Consider this image: We are observing a large river with many smaller rivers and streams flowing into the main estuary. Can you visualize the great main waterway, its vitality and its bustling river traffic? We'll name this river Graphic Design. Now let us look at its tributaries. We will call them packaging, identity, and promotion, all flowing into and merging together to form Graphic Design. The river pilots of these tributaries understand how their water conditions are interrelated with the main river body, but they know their own branches best. The pilots of the main river boats have far-reaching itineraries, traveling up and down all the branching rivers. These pilots enjoy the ever-changing vista and are quite flexible; however, they may have to familiarize themselves anew with waters not often traveled, or they may consult with the local experts. The branch river specialists, however, while aware of the total terrain, find that by limiting themselves to servicing their own river they gain an ever-increased knowledge of its waters. And whenever a traveler needs specific information about their river, the specialists are available for consultation.

This metaphor describes how specialization has evolved within graphic design. In most instances the specialization of these segments has become so highly refined that they have become design businesses with their own strong self-image and marketing strategy. Many of these "marketing communications" firms add to their creative strength by combining strategic planning and research as part of their services.

Meeting the Client's Needs

These areas of specialization are important and necessary in today's complex business community. Graphic design began with and still has many firms practicing a variety of disciplines. For example, let us consider a basic business scenario. We'll assume that graphic design firm A + B Associates has a client, The Widget Corporation. TWC (as The Widget Corporation likes to be called) believes a new logotype to promote its new line of improved widgets will benefit TWC's product introduction, as well as the corporate image. A + B Associates creates the new Widget Identity along with promotional brochures for TWC's sales personnel and customers, in-store banners, posters, counter cards, tee shirts, and buttons with the new logo for employees. It also creates the packaging system for the new Widget line, which will be responsive to the needs of warehouse storage systems, as well as consumer packaging. Everything is so successful that TWC asks A + B Associates to develop an advertising program that will keep the Widget Identity firmly in place in the public's mind and complement the new design system. In addition, new dealer's sales sheets and parts catalogue are assigned to A + B Associates. It's an excellent client/design firm relationship. Every time The Widget Corporation needs anything done, they know just who to call.

That's wonderful, you say. What could possibly be wrong with this picture? Well, nothing. There are many firms that have managed to maintain this sometimes enviable diversity of work. Some of these firms are internationally famous, and many are found in smaller cities such as Seattle or Atlanta. However, the motivating factors producing the current climate of specialization have always been the forces driving the needs of business. When business has grown to certain proportions, many large corporations have a greater comfort level choosing specialized design firms.

Let us once again turn our attention to The Widget Corporation. Eight highly successful years have passed. TWC has increased its output and manufactures fifty-three different consumer products. It also has "gone public" and now is listed on the New York Stock Exchange. TWC has recently diversified by acquiring several other corporations. TWC learns that it needs to court the financial community for funding. It is through the vehicles of its annual reports and quarterly reports that TWC can position the company properly with respect to the stock brokerage houses and the banks. The Widget Corporation's board of directors now believes it may serve the corporation's best interests to seek out a graphic design firm that has a proven track record in dealing with the subtleties of producing such corporate literature. TWC has, additionally, discovered some of its products are losing their market share in the now more complex marketplace. After a consumer research study, TWC's market research firm has recommended a new packaging system that will allow its products to be more visually competitive. TWC clearly needs a firm that understands the research studies, how to interpret the visual criteria, and how to develop a creative strategy that will distinguish TWC's product from the competition. It will seek out a graphic design firm specializing in packaging design. And when TWC comes to believe that its corporate identity system no longer is appropriate for its new position in the marketplace, it seeks out a marketing communications specialist. After strategic analysis, this specialist may not only redesign the old TWC logo but recommend changing TWC's name to something that will not be identified only with widgets but also can be easily adapted to the stock market ticker quotation requirements, adding to its recognition factor.

As you can see, the age of specialization is very much with us for many functional reasons, and indeed, shows no signs of substantially diminishing. Firms that had limited their activities to certain areas of expertise discovered this limitation to be extremely advantageous to their own business. It established them as the experts who solve specific problems. Thus, their reputation grew, identifying them as having the know-how required to fulfill a client's needs, and they in turn became finer-tuned within their specialization. So the restrictiveness feeds upon itself—setting up the dictum: The more specialized work you do, the more you become expert, the more specialized work you get.

Expanding and Diversifying Services

The 1990–1993 recession resulted in a movement toward firms trying to expand their product services. This response to a diminishing source of work was a logical step. Nonetheless, when expansion occurs, it is within the framework of the core business. Conversely, the many firms who had expanded their services during the 1980s to include other business profit centers and branch offices found themselves hurt by the recession. The restructuring pattern of these firms was to sell off or close down business units and return to their original core business.

New media has become the medium that has produced diversity within many design groups. Web design and sometimes CD-ROMs have become an integrated part of projects and have thus created new avenues for creative expression.

With the problem solving tasks required by design firms to meet their client's marketing objectives in mind, and our Widget Corporation as a role model, we will now analyze the individual regions of graphic design, with a look to the future. ■

Identity Design

The core message of this book is that graphic design is a business and various sectors of design are utilized as strategic marketing tools. The design business is unusual due to several factors: it is a service business, its product is creative, and it has no inventory. This statement requires the caveat that in reality, all business is creative and the generalization holds true that any successful business is probably directed by a very creative, entrepreneurial, and innovative individual. Most designers are so caught up in their own creative powers that they fail to recognize this reality. The particularly appealing element of the graphic design business is its output. The product of the service is creative and it is the quality of the design that is the driving force.

With recognition of the vigor and vitality of these factors influencing the business of graphic design, let's now immerse ourselves into the domain of graphic design.

The Identity Business

Identity is image. If there is one essential word we could attach to any part of graphic design or advertising, it is image. We are all in the image business in one way or another. We build, and contribute value to, the image of goods and services for every business imaginable. We do it through perception of the company's graphic "look" and we do it through hard or soft sell, advertising in print and various media. Identity is utilized as a strategic business tool. In graphic design it falls into three basic categories. They are:

- Corporate Identity
- Brand Identity
- Retail Identity

Corporate Identity

Corporate identity is the strategic positioning and creative impact of a company's visual image. Corporate identity has come closer in meaning and perception to central issues of branding, and, in fact, many practitioners prefer using the term *corporate branding*. The usage of corporate branding refers to how the name and visual equity is assimilated by the viewer and all the socio-economic associations incurred by that brand. How that brand is perceived by its clients, public, stockholders, and employees is a crucial element, and CI (corporate identity) is a key marketing tool in every facet of the company's communications. The identity program affects all printed matter, advertising, building signage, trucks, uniforms, promotion materials, packaging, and any other possible conveyance of the corporate image.

Many design firms, large and small, take on identity assignments, and many designers consider themselves practitioners of corporate identity when they create logos and stationery systems. The large and/or highly specialized firms are able to stress in greater detail, and at a far more sophisticated level, the strategic planning components of corporate identity, by utilizing their teams of consultants, nomenclature experts, and account services staff. The scope of these comprehensive and fully realized programs is long term, often taking several years to complete. Such a program requires intensive research and study of the corporate culture, including the firm's past, present, and future perceptions of itself. The process allows the consultant to recommend a strategy that will include evaluation of the company's name, its positioning in the marketplace, future trends analysis, and, finally, its visual image. Note that the visual image is the final result of the strategic positioning, not the first step. To allow the implementation of the image, an extensive identity manual will be created, often produced in an inter-active format, online or by CD-ROM, utilizing technology for its compact and efficient qualities. These manuals set the standards and criteria for all corporate employees who may be in a position to utilize the identity for applications such as publishing, signage, advertising, packaging, or the like.

Therefore, a sophisticated CI practice includes an intensive period of strategic planning, assessment, and inventory of the internal and external operations of the corporation. This "audit" is accomplished by teams composed of the management group as mentioned, consultants, naming and branding experts, account executives, project managers, planners, and graphic designers. This can fluctuate, depending on the personnel available within the consulting firm. In structuring themselves as strategic consultants, many firms utilize a team of key executives comprised of their management consultant group, the marketing staff (who initiated the client contact and sold the project), and the creative director (who develops the core positioning strategy during this "phase 1" period of the project). (In some firms the creative department may be excluded from the first phase of project definition altogether.) For other companies the structure can mean the creative directors assume the account function without any other staff. Other teams are created on as-needed basis with independent consultants. The complexity and sophistication of these company structures and their strategic foci may offer a vastly different perspective to the graphic designer, who tends to think of corporate identity strictly in terms of the visual image.

This management consultant type structure has been gradually expanding for a number of years and presents one of the largest growth areas for personnel. Companies are incorporating in their personnel mix executives—many with MBAs—whose professional experience includes management consulting firms, corporate branding, and advertising. These executives may hold significant positions within the firm, and they work in tandem with the creative group. While the ratio of account services people to creative will vary from firm to firm, and in many large companies the balance is tipped

**Phase 1
Audits**

away from creative, it must be remembered that these firms still deliver a creative product. Their own image as "Marketing Communications" consultants in this instance means operating as image and planning consultants with the visual solution to be determined and executed at the conclusion of the process.

The audit and phase 1 period of CI strategic planning surveys all of the corporation's current visual materials. The audit tracks inconsistencies in the materials, perhaps inconsistencies in logotypes. It is not uncommon for large corporations to have so many divisions functioning independently that over the years the logomark, color, and type can have many variations. This produces a contradictory and disjointed visual message weakening the entire impression of the corporate image. The elimination of duplications in forms and printed materials often save enough money over the long run to justify much of the cost of the CI program. However, this is not the sole motivating factor in a firm's decision to take this route. The reordering of image is far more profound.

The audit's other purpose is to analyze the internal corporate mission. It is as if the audit takes the temperature of the company. By interviewing staff at different levels, the audit learns what the firm thinks of itself, what it believes it wants to accomplish and what it believes it wants to communicate. The end result of the audit should be an extensive profile of the company, emphasizing the perception of the firm from within and from without. The phase 1 procedure can now address the requirements of the new and/or updated image and how best to communicate this revitalized image.

Nomenclature

The first phase of the new or revised vision of the corporation will address the firm's name. Does the name still communicate what the consensus believes the company represents? Should the name be changed subtlety or dramatically? The issue of "equity" becomes a major factor. Equity means how readily a name, its logotype, and corporate message are recognized by the public. If the recognition factor is very strong there may be less tampering with its intrinsic character and emphasis may be placed on modernization or establishing an updated look. These are the essential questions that must be answered at this stage. *The protection of equity is a fundamental consideration in any name or image change.* Naming is a key component of the corporate branding process and is most often identified as nomenclature. Name changes are common with mergers, and mergers represent a key market for new corporate identity business. When companies are merged or acquired, something, if not everything, will need to be changed. Nomenclature is part of a corporate identity firm's services and the firm employs staff experts. There are also many independent nomenclature specialists who function as naming and branding consultants.

There are some interesting examples of excellent work by the nomenclature experts, and some extremely bad choices as well. For example, Sperry Rand was a merger of the Sperry and Rand corporations. Then the name was shortened to Sperry. When Sperry and Burrows merged the result was Unysis. This name was the result of a company contest for a new name. Some names are developed in response to their symbol on the stock market. Nobody refers to IBM as International Business Machines. Citicorp was The City Bank of New York until it determined its mission was to become an international bank. FedEx (naming and identity by Landor Associates) and KFC (by Interbrand Schechter) represent the triumph of usage over the "real" names of Federal Express and Kentucky Fried Chicken. Name changes are also sensitive to the needs of electronic sites and the resulting designs are sensitive to the needs of animation on these sites. Spin-offs cause the need for new names and identities. Lucent Technologies (Landor Associates) represents a spin-off of AT&T. A company's need to position itself in the changing marketplace can create a name change. Such a total name change was accomplished by Rochester Telephone when the firm Diefenbach Elkins took it from a regional telephone company to a national provider of information and communications services. The resulting name is Frontier. The naming of products and the relationship to new product development dovetails with branding efforts. As new products (branding), corporations, or business services are developed and introduced, the name chosen is the essential component of the recognition factor.

It is only after all of these studies that the graphic designer can delve into the visual systems that will provide the

Visual Systems

solutions needed. Systems design is what a lot of identity design is all about. It is the operable visual systems that will bring clarity and order to the strategy of image.

Once the system is designed, the paramount need is to implement the program with adequate quality control. If the program is not scrupulously administered by the corporation, it will eventually fall into disarray and create many of the same problems that triggered the CI program's initiation. Should the firm be large and widespread, controlling the identity program can be a full-time task. The consultant may introduce training programs for various managers within the company and will probably suggest the need for a design management director for corporate identity (if there isn't a person in place already). Often, this experience will provide CI designers a career segue to the corporate side as design managers. The vehicle that will control the level of standards to be maintained is the corporate identity manual.

Corporate Identity Manuals

The manuals can cover a wide range in style and size as well. Some traditional master manuals are composed of encyclopedic binders with sections devoted to every possible condition in which a logo system could be applied, indicating the correct and incorrect methods of application and including precise color charts. The manual is extremely explicit, containing diagrams and many visual examples of accurate methods of placing the mark or logomark onto advertisements, forms, checks, signage, brochures, and trucks. The manual may also include camera-ready typography in different point sizes. Segments of manuals can be separated out to address specific sections of the whole picture. Such segments are distributed only to those corporate divisions which will find them applicable. Some manuals use proprietary software to disseminate the required information.

Corporate identity manuals have taken the inevitable turn toward computerization. These information vehicles can be easily disseminated via CD-ROM or intranet services within a company or sectioned out as needed to specific departments in any part of the world, offering the opportunity to deliver information to clients in an interactive, technically friendly manner that also provides the receiver with the proper tools to make individual decisions.

The designer's role in corporate identity is to graphically crystallize the corporate image. That image was determined through the deep introspection of the phase 1 analysis. The conclusion of a successful identity program significantly effects the general health of the corporation. The graphic designer who can apply his/her talent to create meaningful design systems will find this field very rewarding.

Retail Identity

Retail Identity (RI) works in the same manner as corporate identity and is often a part of a comprehensive CI program. In recent years, it has become a separate area because of the rise of an important and large market in specialty retailing. Initially, retail was considered just another form of CI and much of its business was (and, in some cases, still is) funneled through standard CI departments. While most people generally associate retail with shops and stores, it can also mean gas stations, banking centers, ATMs (automatic teller machine stations), and anything you would find in a shopping mall or airport.

This form of identity establishes the marketing image of the retail environment (environmental design strongly dovetails and sometimes includes retail identity). It duplicates the strategic planning of corporate identity, but the specialized focus is on retail marketing. Therefore, how the retail image is designed and marketed to the public is the designer's mission. The design may start with a logotype but will extend to the layout of the environment (again, possibly working with environmental designers), banners, shopping bags, signage, and packaging.

Brand Identity and Packaging Design

Branding and packaging can rarely be separated. Traditionally, many packaging design firms were only involved with the package itself. As the significance of the design's effect on the product's marketing was recognized, design firms began to participate in the total image of the product (hence, designing the brand image). For our purposes, however, let's separate the two.

Branding or brand identity (BI) simply deals with the logotype and naming of the product. However, it is far from a simple imaging problem, for the brand equity (the same "equity" factor as discussed in corporate identity) is the most important instrument of the marketing strategy. *If that equity is to be changed, it has to be done in a manner that will not destroy, but enhance the history of that equity.* A classic example would be a study of the Coca-Cola or Pepsi-Cola logo and how each has slowly and gradually changed over the years. These visual images are the icons of our culture. The subtle changes are testimony to how incremental the updates are over the years and, most importantly, the need to make changes without the public's awareness and yet with their acceptance of the product as contemporary. Updating an image without changing the equity of the old is the key to branding. Sometimes changes to the visual image are a result of a marketing strategy in trouble. When Pepsi developed its campaign of a young, trendy drink (The Pepsi Generation), making Coke look stodgy, Coke responded with Classic Coke. It resulted in one of the best marketing/branding solutions possible. And while the packaging returned updated variations of the original bottle, the strategy also allowed for an enormous variety in Coke packaging design.

It is usually estimated that a brand and package have a life span of perhaps eight years, at which point they may need to be updated. Those guidelines have been re-analyzed in our fast and faster society and products are being updated on a quicker timetable. The significant word that must be stressed is "update."

Product Equity The equity of a product and name is the reputation and goodwill of that product. The equity of a corporation or product is the essential marketing tool challenging the designer. You can be sure the corporation's product managers are very cautious to protect any changes that might challenge the image's equity as revealed in the product's positioning and market share. *Graphic designers must learn the company's marketing strategy before they can begin to tamper with the design. They must be able to communicate on equal terms with the brand and product managers.* These are the classic MBA (Master of Business Administration) folk who, chances are, have never taken a design course, just as designers rarely have access to marketing in their undergraduate curricula. While the problems inherent in this situation are clear (and although a graduate program in Design Management has recently been developed at Pratt Institute, one wonders when the general curriculum in design education will include these important issues), these two constituents are in partnership and must work as a team to bring the solutions to fruition. The graphic designer must recognize that the path to success requires communication with the marketing and business powers that be. While both designer and marketer should learn in this process, the designer must aggressively absorb the appropriate marketing language and savvy to achieve the established goals.

Packaging design has had a powerful impact on the advertising and marketing of consumer products, since it has long been recognized as the last point of communication with the consumer. Advertising's role is to condition the individual's product perception (for example, how you feel about a product). It also establishes its status and identifies its audience. Advertising can promote a product or offer incentives to buy the product. It is packaging, however, that performs the former (the product must be ready to show in the ads) and latter task of presentation to the consumer.

Shelf Impact

The package communicates in advertising when an image of it is displayed in tandem with the advertising copy in print ads. However, its strongest impact is on the shelf. It is in the retailer's arena that the package must stand out against its competition. The marketing researcher's role is to control the focus groups and research studies to determine how the product is perceived and accepted by the public. Does the package (and the advertising) send the message determined by the corporate marketing and product managers? Is the color, design, size, and positioning of the branding correct? The designer's priority is to manipulate these elements to solve and precisely communicate these objectives. The package becomes a three-dimensional advertisement and it operates at the last place of consumer resistance or impulse— the crucial moment the consumer reaches for the product on the shelf.

Packaging design also consists of many technical elements that the graphic designer needs to know. There is the physical structure of the package itself. The materials, printing, and engineering are some of the elements tangential to the design. Product or industrial designers, as well as packaging engineers, can provide the three-dimensional design needed. In addition, the designer is currently faced with concerns about ecology, and must decide how to eliminate unnecessary boxes and how to use environmentally safe materials and

Physical Structure

IDENTITY DESIGN

printing processes. The so-called "green" movement or "green" packaging denotes an effort toward ecologically sound packaging. It is a movement that first gained momentum in England around 1989. Corporations are embracing the concept, and consumer awareness of ecological needs is rising. When corporations believe "green" packaging and "green" products will generate marketing benefits due to consumer acceptance, use of such packaging and products will accelerate. It will certainly be a force in marketing and design for the future. Federal regulations have also mandated changes in packaging labeling. How the size, actual content, nutritional elements, and ingredients are displayed are now controlled under The Nutrition Labeling and Education Act of 1990, which mandated compliance by 1994. All these factors challenge the graphic designer's ability to create a successful design that is responsive to the criteria established by the client.

Packaging design, like all the divisions of graphic design, has experienced rapid computerization, and, therefore, the restructuring of its work force. The Apple Macintosh environment is the market standard and design firms are on line. They are able to complete color and layout variations at speeds unknown before. They are also very successful in implementing the line extensions as required. Line extensions contain the modifications for a product's variations, such as a jam line whose label will change color with different flavors, or a shampoo that requires different labels for dry or oily, scented or unscented.

Computerization of Design

The computerization of design firms has created another, more substantive change in the emerging character of these firms, which divides them into two distinct groups. First, firms that can manage the required strategic planning and product positioning are moving to the forefront of industry leadership. These firms' projects are the large national and multinational brands with many SKU's (Stock Keeping Units, a count of every unit of change in a product's size or line extension, such as how many units are spun off a single product). Secondly, there are many small design groups, perhaps less than ten people, who work on smaller brands or less complicated projects. Computerization has made these firms fast and nimble. There are also numerous individuals who, with their own computer installations, can work from home either on freelance projects or for other design firms, often transmitting the work by modem. This is a particular boon to those with young families. Computerization has also caused a particular challenge to the field in relationship to changes in the pricing structures. The pricing of projects and the demand for speed has the negative effect of turning the work of these firms into a commodity, an item that is purchased on the premise of delivery on time for the lowest price. The positive result of this challenge is that larger firms are forced to offer value-added services associated with strategic planning, along with the graphic expertise, through their staffing of consultants and account services. These firms therefore become powerful marketing consultancies, offering a broader range of services and playing a far more important role in the development of a product than simply design.

Packaging design has the enviable attribute of being almost recession-proof. In difficult economic times corporations may not earmark funds for research, development, and new products, and they may cut back on their advertising budgets. But they do recognize that certain products will be bought, no matter what. How will they command control of the consumer at the point of purchase? Through the package. History has proven that while design firms can be downsized, they rarely let go of their prized designers. They find other ways to economize. My experience has shown there has always been a market for excellent packaging design talent.

Successful packaging designers develop such savvy in marketing that their career paths become quite flexible with many options. After years of apprenticeship and experience in design firms, many find their futures may include not only becoming a key player with possible equity in their firm, but the ability to transfer their skills to the corporate sector. They can assume positions within corporations in design management. Design management positions usually entail managing product lines from the creative point of view within the corporation. Design managers rarely have hands-on creative responsibilities, but rather manage the process by working in liaison with the corporation's product and marketing groups, as well as controlling the creative process by supervising design studios and vendors. Design managers must be able to make critical taste judgements, articulate marketing objectives, and work within the corporate environment. Some other designers go on from their creative responsibilities to take management positions stressing

Career Paths

strategic planning, account services, or new business development. Some prefer to operate small, independent design firms or to become permanent freelancers. The required skill and specialized knowledge of packaging establishes their value, whichever direction they choose. ■

Print Design

This is a vast area, attracting designers who love print. In its simplest form, print design includes any printed materials that are two-dimensional, such as pamphlets, brochures, posters, and various other published materials. The semantics of the communication fields can sometimes be confusing. In advertising, "print" refers to ads—print advertising—as opposed to advertising on television or film. And in advertising, "collateral" refers to many of the projects designers call "print," such as brochures and other printed materials separate from ads.

For our purposes, the following areas are included in the context of print design.

Corporate Literature

Corporate literature is so broad it can include every and all forms of brochures, annual reports, sales tools, and promotional print. It includes companies whose products may be business-to-business services, financial or technical services, or consumer products. It speaks to all sectors of the economy. Editorial design plays a role as well, as many firms have company magazines and newsletters. The field of corporate communications is dominated by the need to produce a vast variety of print materials whose audience is both within and without the corporation.

Print design has suffered in recent years the stigma of being too "design-y," that designers make things look too "pretty." Indeed, there have been many examples of design becoming so precious and so self-involved that it fails to communicate. The challenge is to overcome the perception that designers are only communicating with their peers. The obsession with texture or typography manipulated by computer to the point illegibility helps support this observation. Trendy design clichés rarely solve real and pragmatic communications problems, although many experimental designers have produced a body of work that can influence others to newer ways of expression. When the visual does not communicate the message, the public and the designer's clients can become confused or dissatisfied. Designers may have pursued a cutting-edge image but if the work didn't serve basic communication needs, the chances are the client moved on.

Information Design/Informational Architecture

Print design, like every other sector of the communications field, has to be responsive to the marketing and informational needs of the project. *Information is the operative word for whatever mode of print we discuss.* Its mission is to inform about products and communicate the image and ideas of the corporation. Information design became one of the buzzwords of the early 1990s as businesses consistently moved toward developing systems to manage the mounting volume of information, learning how to incorporate various media to offer clients the best deliverable choices while maintaining clarity of design and proper usage of information. The dissemination of clear, logical information is the challenge facing every designer in a world that is deluged with too much information to absorb. Design must confront the necessity to develop systems that deliver an understandable message. The organization of information and verbal or visual material is essential to the process. Information architecture, identified by Richard Saul Wurman, refers to the designer's role as the manager of information—a term preferred by some to that of graphic design.

Clement Mok, the Creative Director of Studio Archetype, also referred to Wurman's role in pointing designers toward information architecture in his book *Designing Business*. He stated:

> The economy is now based on a vast system of knowledge created by the merging of technologies, information, and media. In the past, knowledge systems were in the domain of information services managers and information scientists (otherwise known as librarians) whose professions weren't highly esteemed because of their focus on organizing data, rather than creating it. Now, small chunks of data appear in high-speed conglomerations, and they're often unedited and have no identifiable connection to original sources. It's little wonder the media explosion perplexes people.
>
> Information architecture, the meaningful organization of information, is becoming an important discipline because it concentrates on deciphering data and giving it shape within the complex structure behind the computer screen. The Edward Tuftes and Richard Wurmans of ten or fifteen years ago were correct in their prediction that people would begin paying close attention to information science.
>
> Today, information is a product. When information is in the right hands, it can be translated through design into powerful products and services—and successful businesses.

The designer must also develop the skills to analyze and conceive what the message should be. In order to achieve this goal a designer needs to be concerned with all aspects of the message, not just the visual. The designer has the ability to provide the pivotal role by recommending concept, content, and strategy, along with design.

Copywriting is the vehicle through which information and the message is often delivered. *Copy is the conceptual partner to the visual solution and copy is the key component with which designers must work.* In the past, copy was associated only with advertising. Not so today.

There is an old perception among advertising agency folk that designers are not conceptual. In their viewpoint designers only know how to make things look good (and of course they know all about typefaces and computers), but they are basically not conceptual the way advertising is. The concept is not often expressed to designers, and when it is, it is greeted with understandable shock. This notion is perhaps admissible for those who deal only with the purer elements of design. It certainly is not valid for the designer who understands the value, meaning, and necessity of copy as the force directing the visual interpretation. Another aspect of this parochial view is the differentiation within advertising between art and copy. While they both are integral functions of the creative, and while art directors and copywriters work as teams, advertising has traditionally been copy-driven. When an agency needs to hire a creative director, its request will often acknowledge an ambivalence as to whether the person has an art or copy background. But, in fact, when the decision-making process is over, the position usually goes to the copywriter. It's a bewildering fact to most art directors. Why does this happen? Because the message, and therefore the essential concept, is most often in the copy. The sooner art directors and designers begin to think of this total picture of integrated art and copy, the better.

Informational Design

Informational design is semantically a variant of information design, an interesting career tangent, and a combination of print design and systems design. Information systems and systems design have been applied to the design of forms, legal documents, and publications stressing facts. Guide books, instruction manuals, charts, graphs, newspaper, and television informational visuals are all important regions for this work. The applications to the interactive forms of multimedia, user interface, and icon design for software are easily apparent (See chapter 8). It is a growing area of graphic design that offers the tremendous value of clarity in a society on information overload. It also demands and requires the analysis of information and for that information to then be designed and delivered in a clear, logical manner. The needs of the audience must always be served and the information kept "consumer friendly."

The New York design firm Siegel & Gale opened a new frontier in graphic design when it developed Language Simplification in 1975. It came as a response to a need for clarity of business forms, both in their visual appearance and their written language. Alan Siegel was the first to recognize the opportunity to pair the work of graphic designers with attorneys to produce loan forms, all kinds of applications, and even the redesign of federal tax forms for the United States and Canadian governments. The work has proven fascinating to designers who have an interest in combining their typographical skills with systems design, and Language Simplification has also benefitted the public in a measurable way.

Informational design is most appropriate for designers who thrive on analytical and organizational systems and typography. These are only a few examples as the field has yet to be fully explored. These skills can also be transferred and utilized in exhibition design.

Annual Reports

This highly specialized field is another example of an area that requires creative talent skilled to meet the needs of marketing corporate communications. The annual report is a mandated corporate year-end report and has grown into a significant marketing tool for those publicly held corporations that need to attract investors. The Federal Security and Exchange Commission mandates that all publicly held corporations issue annual reports to their stockholders. In addition, many choose to issue quarterly reports.

These materials have become informational guidebooks to the corporation. They not only communicate the image and economic health of the organization, but have come to express how the organization feels about itself and its future. The annual report is significant not only because it is distributed to the stockholders, but also because it is a marketing tool for the financial sector (Wall Street) to attract future investors and employees. It is an instrument of research for anyone who wants in-depth information on the company. The annual report can contain a story line or interviews with employees or customers. Since the report's role so strongly relies on image, it has become one of the corporation's most significant communications devices. The point of view in the written copy as well as the visual image can narrate a far more focused message than reading the mandatory financial

Communicating Corporate Image

information in the back of the book. It's the company's annual opportunity to communicate its story. Even a superficial look at a random selection of annual reports will quickly reveal their vastly divergent viewpoints. A closer look will confirm that this is a highly sophisticated medium of corporate communications.

The financial information submitted by the corporation has to be scrutinized carefully for accuracy. The overriding message as well as the company's depiction has to be approved by the CEO and president. Sometimes the very nature of the annual report can trigger an overly obsessive case of collective corporate paranoia. I remember a time when a designer had to insert and remove a single comma some fifteen times. The designer is in partnership with the top echelon of the firm and the whole enterprise's responsibility rests on few shoulders. It can be a tense time, with the designer in a pivotal position.

Annual reports have also come to be a design status symbol for the corporation. For some companies, much emphasis is placed on the quality of the image they wish to portray. When reports win coveted prizes, the prize goes to the corporation as well as the design firm. While the pressure exists to get the job done right and on time, the freedom to use the report as a creative medium is considerable in some cases. Huge budgets can be riding on large printings. Only the very best photographers and illustrators will do. The quality of paper and printing became paramount. These priorities can be hard to duplicate in other avenues of print design. The result is often an enviable work.

Graphic designers who work within this area can realize a meaningful and well-compensated career. The key is having the staying power, for too often there is a significant burnout

Workplace Demands factor. This is caused by changes in content, delays, and the fact that the majority of annual reports are subject to strict deadlines. Reports coincide with the company's annual meeting and usually appear early in March. As a consequence, these deadlines produce a fairly seasonal business in which the bulk of the work is done between Labor Day and April 15. Most firms are attempting to structure their businesses into a twelve-month year. Some annuals do not have the April 15 deadline, and firms are also able to develop other design products.

During these deadline periods studios can work very long

hours, six to seven days a week. Then there is the need to go "on press," to supervise the printing, make any last-minute decisions, and make sure it is as "perfect" as possible. While press time is reserved in advance, of course there are always last minute emergencies. It seems everyone I have ever known has ended up on press at two A.M. in some small town somewhere in the United States. You can understand why people get burned out and may want to leave this specialized field. But when you look at the really great reports, you can also understand why there are those who are totally dedicated to this work.

Corporate Communications

This identifier is usually used for corporate materials that are often, but not exclusively, accomplished by an in-house corporate staff. These are the communications products that serve to promote the corporation. They can include, but are not limited to, capability brochures, annual reports, company newsletters, sales tools, internal company forms, posters, invitations, special events announcements, logomarks for subsidiary divisions, multimedia materials, sales meeting materials, incentive awards, and company magazines. The communications sector of a corporation may also work with the assigned advertising agency if there is not one in-house. Few corporations do their own advertising.

Designers working within a corporation usually have a very different experience than those working for a marketing communications firm or design studio. The biggest difference is that, while the designer may have many corporate divisions as "clients," there is really only one client. This is one of those good news/bad news tradeoffs. The diversity of many clients is found in design consultancies but chances are it will be a specialized consultancy. The corporation may offer only one very large client and the diversity comes from having to do virtually everything for that client.

Working for a corporation used to mean substantial job security. While that notion has changed with the economic turmoil of the last decade, the turnover in corporate positions is still much lower than in the offices of design consultants. Corporations are slower to hire and slower to fire. The atmosphere is traditionally conservative. Corporate positions are highly prized for their excellent benefit programs, shorter work weeks, and relative security. Obviously, since corporations are located all over the country, the ability to relocate is a necessity.

Editorial Design

Editorial design refers to the design of magazines. It must be remembered that magazines currently appear in print as well as in on-line media. The publishing field is not the only market for editorial designers, as many special interest groups and corporations will develop books and magazines as part of their corporate communications effort. It works much like other areas we have discussed, except the "client" is the publisher and/or editor. The audience is the public at large.

Publishing is, of course, the core for editorial design and it is a field in which the publishers and editors make the primary decisions relating to the focus, concept, and marketing of the product. They hire the creative director and/or art director who can work with them to visualize their publication's point of view. A creative director is usually necessary when a publication is very large or there are several publications within a group. Otherwise, the top creative title is usually senior art director or art director. Under the creative head is a creative group whose size depends on the size of the publication and how often it is published. A weekly publication requires more effort than a monthly. This group may, therefore, include an associate art director, assistant art director, designers, and production artists. It is always valuable to check the mastheads of magazines, for they will credit the staff and this allows you to see the structure. The creative director or art director will be responsible for hiring the staff, which can also include photo stylists or photo editors. The distinction between an art director's responsibility and a designer's is reflected in their roles. The art director "directs" the creative team on staff, the photo shoots, and the illustrators, and generally functions as a person who makes creative decisions in a supervisory manner. The designer is primarily involved with the hands-on implementation of those decisions, working on the layout (mostly with software programs), and perhaps makes some of the type and visuals decisions. The designer's responsibilities will vary, depending upon the size of the staff and how much the art director may wish to delegate. If the publication's staff is small enough, the art director may be asked to do the work of a designer as well. Designers are hired because of their ability to understand the subject matter and visually realize the magazine editor's focus. When designers change jobs, it is also easier to move within a subject matter. For example, high fashion and financial publications are so far apart in their content that most often a switch from one to the other is not possible.

Magazines fall into specialized business categories. They are:

- Lifestyle (such as a regional, like *New York* magazine)
- Fashion
- Business
- Trade (not found on newsstands)
- High tech (computers, science)
- Consumer and special interest (computers, automotive, children, education, travel, health and fitness, entertainment, financial)

Editorial promotion is often integrated within the editorial department. Magazine promotion can mean rate cards, subscription inserts, and promotional brochures, computer floppy disks and kits geared to attract advertisers. While we discuss promotion separately, it is necessary to point out how often it is closely linked with the editorial. The publisher will, of necessity, have a keen interest in the magazine's effective promotion. In addition, on small publications, the art direction staff may be called upon to design or supervise the promotion as well as the magazine.

Book Design

Book design is often perceived in relation to the design of book jackets. While this is the most visible, and in some ways splashy, manifestation of the design work, it is far from the whole story. The layout of the total book is a subject that requires insight into the character and purpose of the book. It requires establishing in the layout a sensitivity toward systems design and informational design, as well as a deep concern for typography. Often the design responsibilities will be separated, with one person responsible for the cover and another person for the interior. Art directors will originate the overall concept and then choose the appropriate illustrators, photographers, and typographers to achieve their vision.

The book publishing field falls into many specialized categories within the separations of hard cover, soft cover, and paperback. They include:

- Textbooks
- Fiction/nonfiction
- Children's publications
- Trade publications
- Special interest (travel, cookbooks, etc.)

Book Packagers

Book packagers occupy an interesting corner of the publishing field. They sometimes group publications together based on compatibility of subject matter or perhaps package a promotional device along with the book. A common example of a packaged publication grouping would be "The Collected Works of. . . ." More inventive packages can offer an aligned product such as the well-known illustrator Geoffrey Moss's wonderful children's book *Henry's Moon* (packaged by Sommerville House in conjunction with Little Brown Publishing), which included a night light with a shade that was an illustration from the book.

Interactive Publishing

Publishing's utilization of new technologies has created several important new directions. The CD-ROM offers an interactive form of publishing, containing not only a replica of the print version but also the ability to involve the reader as an active decision maker in choosing information in a dialogue with the subject. It is, after all, nothing more than putting published material on an interactive screen, but the inherent qualities of the interactive process (this interrelates to information found in chapters 7 and 8) produce a wonderful learning device. Instructions for playing better tennis, visiting a museum, or learning about history can be more effective in this format. It's a business that will create many new jobs for designers, as each option on the screen requires another layout. Within the textbook area, it is now possible to customize textbooks to meet teachers' specialized requirements. Books are being designed with flexible formats so that an instructor can request a text containing specific chapters from different source books. The final, customized text can be delivered on short notice and with the instructor's name on the cover.

Book design positions exist primarily within publishing firms, but a large number of assignments are distributed to small studios and freelancers. For creative directors or art directors, the practice of assigning projects facilitates the design flexibility required by vastly different subject matter. Hiring outside talent allows total design adaptability. ■

5

Environmental Design

This area is an amalgam of two-dimensional and three-dimensional design, and so it attracts industrial designers, architects, interior designers, as well as graphic designers. It is an emerging discipline, and allows designers to work in many diversified ways, and usually with a expanded team of creative people. Environmental design represents a mosaic of design specialties, and therefore stands alone, unique in this capacity. The identifier "environmental" does not pertain to ecological concerns. This is a semantical confusion that sometimes causes the mistaken belief that an environmental designer is working on projects to clean up our environment.

A Definition

It is difficult to give a narrow definition of environmental design because it is a broadly based discipline. Many retail design and industrial design characteristics apply to this field as well, and environmental design projects attract designers from both areas. Environmental design is gaining recognition as a specialized design field as designers gain experience with the specific problems encountered in working on environmental projects. The focus of this design area is on design projects of interior and exterior spaces, often in relationship to a larger environment. Environmental designers are not architects responsible for a total structure. They can, however, work with architects to produce spaces that usually incorporate the usage of graphic design as well. A sampling of the kinds of projects that the environmental designer can administer would include: retail marketing, store planning, shopping mall design, airport facilities, hotel spaces, office building lobbies, all signage projects, parks, zoos, subways, and exhibition design.

Where Environmental Designers Work

Most positions are found in small (less than twenty-five people) design consultancies. These firms will usually request a specific area of involvement, such as an exhibition designer or, perhaps, a signage designer. Nonetheless, the work and skills required are quite flexible.

Corporations occasionally utilize environmental designers, most often in the retail areas (store planners, display, etc.), or in massive theme park developments (see Licensing, chapter 6). Walt Disney's Imagineering division in Burbank, California is a premier example, employing a very large staff of environmental designers and conceptualizers who work in a think-tank environment utilizing exhibition designers, illustrators, model makers, graphic designers, industrial designers, and signage specialists. In addition, landscape architects are sometimes a source for signage projects.

In any discussion of environmental design the relationship to industrial design and industrial design education is very important. (Please see chapter 7, Industrial Design.)

Sample Projects

Perhaps a look at the 1995 Society of Environmental Graphic Designers (SEGD) award-winning projects is a way to understand the scope of environmental design. The awards for design merit included: A/X: Armani Exchange, New York City; Field Museum of Chicago, Circulation & Wayfinding Master Plan; New York Public Library, Identity & Centennial

Graphics; University Center Environmental Identity, Balti-
more; Houston Uptown Streetscape, Houston; Grand Central
Station, New York City, XIX Amendment Installation in
Main Waiting Room; Sony Plaza, New York City; Apple
Exhibit Expansion Program, Comdex, Las Vegas; Duncan
Aviation Tradeshow Exhibition, Las Vegas; Amtrak Graphic
Signage Standards Manual Corporate Offices; and the Rock
and Roll Hall of Fame, Cleveland.

This list indicates not only the range of the projects but
also the scale. It is no wonder this area of design is gaining in
recognition. Colleges are beginning to include environmental
design in their curriculum and designers are becoming more
enthusiastic about entering this expanding field.

Advice from Two Great Designers

Louis Nelson, IDSA, SEGD, AIGA, has many project to
his credit, the most recent of which is the Korean War Memorial in Washington, DC. I asked him what he would say to a
young designer interested in environmental design. Here is
his response:

Spaces for people.

The challenge today is not too different from the challenge of yesterday—make it beautiful and make it meaningful. Today, achieving this goal only appears more difficult
because expectations are higher (for some, maybe lower), the
playing field is costlier, some of the players are bigger, and
fewer customers and clients are willing to take the necessary
risk—to the curious point that most everything in a category
looks surprisingly the same. Yet, everyone wants something
different.

Today, I tell my staff, and myself, "make it beautiful,
make it reach the heart of the people, make it original."
Make it absolutely desirable to touch, to pick up, to own, to
experience—to possess. Make it mean something to people
emotionally, physically, psychically, practically. Learn about
people and what they need. Understand the clues behind
their actions, word, and gestures. See into their hearts and
guts and minds.

Give it its own personality so that nothing else is like it.
We remember a personality. Environments are created by

many professions. The truly good ones are created by artist-designers in touch with people, whether it's a subway station, restaurant, museum, airport terminal, or a national memorial.

So, looking ahead is really looking at today. Regardless of the new millennium and the forecasts for higher technology, greater interactivity on the Web, bigger crowds, and the search for more instant success, my task is to keep the focus on the principles in my heart and gut. Amidst the noise, here is the challenge.

Nancye Green closes this chapter with both excellent advise and a view towards the future. Nancye is trained as a graphic designer. She and her husband Michael Donnovan head Donnovan & Green (just acquired by CKS Partners). They have completed projects for a diversity of clients including Hallmark, Texas Instruments, The Regan Library, and Hoffman-LaRoche. I asked her: How would she define today's challenge?

The greatest challenge I find working today is how much you really need to know to solve even the simplest problem presented. The designer has to bring design skills to the work, as well as a sophisticated understanding of what is going on in the world that affects the behavior of audiences and consumers, and is critical to the evolving landscape of any business. In environmental design this is further compli-cated by the number of design disciplines that many envi-ronmental design projects draw upon...graphic design, industrial design, interior design, and architecture, not to mention a host of media/electronic possibilities. So, while environmental designers need to understand their clients' businesses, they also need to be intelligent about a broad range of media which are being redefined almost daily.

How would she advise people entering this area of business?

Get smart! Learn about the craft you intend to practice. But also keep up with what's going on in the world. Technology is certainly important. As important are the big trends that are affecting the clients' businesses you serve as well as their customers lives.

And what future did she see in her crystal ball?

Designers will be important organizers of experiences and information to be delivered through an increasing number of media, distributed across a wider range of channels. Instead of designing one thing which reaches many, we will be creating systems in which personalized messages and experiences will be possible. We have to think of ourselves not only as creators of objects, but as using our intelligence and discipline to design processes and systems. This is a profound change! ■

Promotional Design

Promotion represents an exceptionally broad area, one probably least known to most young designers, and yet it offers the largest number of employment opportunities. Sales promotion is also the place where design and advertising meet. Therefore, an understanding of marketing strategies, copywriting, and marketing communications is necessary. The promotional designer has to connect these elements to produce a printed piece that will cry out for attention and sell an idea, service, or product.

Integrated Advertising and Design

We have touched on many of the differences between design and advertising. It must be noted, however, that as the advertising world has become decentralized and more diversified, there are many firms that are true hybrids of these two disciplines. This is a new breed of agency which is generally smaller and stresses a type of problem solving that breaks down barriers and stereotypes. These companies are exciting. However, while their work will utilize and emphasize an impactful design element, in many cases it is still conceptual advertising. Other similar groups are the divisions within many large advertising agencies which are devoted to sales promotion or marketing communications. These groups require the talent of designers who can think of marketing strategies. It is an opportunity for the designer who wants the challenge of thinking on a different scale.

Some of these firms are philosophically wed to the concept of *integrated marketing*. Integrated marketing is a method of approaching a communications problem from the most sensible point of view. The strategy may combine a package of various media for the client to promote his goods or services in a variety of ways. These packages may include promotional design, traditional advertising, packaging design, direct marketing, or special events. Many large advertising agencies, who have subsidiary divisions, attempt to provide integrated services, but at this point in time they are just beginning to break new ground.

Sales Promotion

Although the premise is similar to advertising, it must be remembered that promotion is not print advertising. Sales promotion is printed matter that can be in the form of brochures, sales kits, sell sheets, rate cards, point-of-sale displays (POS—or sometimes called point of purchase, POP—as seen in super-markets, drugstores, banks, or any other retail establishments), banners, and posters. Special promotional gifts can come in the form of kits, boxes, special events marketing, and sales giveaways (such as kits, tee shirts, buttons, matchbooks, hats, and menus), or contests, sweepstakes, and other incentive offerings (special mailers, posters, and displays). Within the publishing field we can find special inserts in magazines (for subscriptions, mail-aways) and magazines advertorials (editorial inserts sponsored by an advertiser). Many package goods companies will offer free standing inserts (FSIs are coupons, often part of an ad, inserted in newspapers and magazines). Outdoor promotions include billboards and posters on mass transit or bus shelters. The cosmetic and fragrance market has made special promotions of gift-with-purchase and purchase-with-purchase (GWP and PWP, as they are prevalently known) a way of life in department stores. They also utilize special mailers distinct from, but sometimes similar to, direct marketing advertising.

Promotional Firms

As you can see, promotion covers a vast area. The products promoted can include anything that is marketed throughout the world. This accounts for its huge diversity. To understand how broad-based promotion is, apply these items (all of which have to be designed) to the diversity of companies needing these services. Think about all the sales promotion generated by an IBM. The product categories: sales tools for sales personnel; giveaway information for the consumer; trade shows for marketers and retailers with their trinkets of balloons, pens, and disks; the retail outlets' need for display cards, posters, signage; the promotions for a charity or cause (fund raising, ecology, etc.); the awards given to distinguished personnel (gift and travel incentives, as well as trophies and awards); and materials for corporate sales conventions (programs, name tags, and menus). Now consider what it might be like handling the promotion for a television network: developing sales kits to promote sponsorship of specific programs (promoting the time buying), enticing affiliate stations into airing specific shows (which are "leased" from the network), or creating consumer awareness (on-air promotional spots). If you were working for a fragrance/cosmetic company you would develop many of these same products but with a completely different image and point of view.

The diversity is enormous and underrated as an avenue for career opportunities. I've often felt sales promotion is an unknown field in the minds of young designers, for it certainly has a very low recognition factor. It may not be the most glamorous design work, but it can be a lot of fun and does offer a significant number of employment opportunities.

Where Are the Promotion Jobs?

Promotion can be produced by design studios as well as in-house corporate groups. Most publishing firms devise a large sales promotion effort. The balance between design done within a company and the amount given to outside studios or agencies is a pendulum whose swings are dependent on the economic times and mood. Many advertising agencies have traditionally had sales promotion groups within the agency. When they are part of the internal structure of the agency they work for the same clients as the agency. The agency does the print advertising, radio, and television. The promotion group does anything else required by the client, from packaging design to cookbooks. Many of these groups have been spunoff as separate profit centers, perhaps with different names that may or may not be directly associated with the agency name. These spin-offs occur to allow the promotional group to seek clients different from the parent company without causing a conflict of client interests. For example, an agency might have a banking client, which would prevent them from working for another financial institution. However, a separate promotional design group could pitch other financial services clients, promoting their expertise in that area. Advertising agency promotional groups are, in many cases, the "diversified studios" that many designers desire. The downside is that often the quality of design produced by many agencies is mediocre. While some agency sales promotion divisions do exceedingly fine work, the general level is below that of design firms. Perhaps this is explained by the general agency business focus on producing work for television spots. Promotion has traditionally been a "step child" department. As these groups now are becoming more attractive profit centers and the focus shifts, the quality should improve. The key to quality is determined by the quality of the client and what the client demands, regardless of where the work is done.

Licensing

This area of design has expanded greatly in the past few years and offers a whimsical, fun side to graphics. Its essence is close to that of sales promotion. Producing products with images to promote a personality or idea dates back to ancient times. While the Romans sold souvenirs at gladiator fights, no one could foresee the ubiquitous effect of sports and entertainment marketing in this century. Today the team identifying logos and mascots for the National Football

League or National Basketball Association, for example, have generated a complex, multi-billion dollar industry. The marketing gurus have discovered that almost anything can be sold with a famous character or slogan such as Garfield, Batman, The Simpsons, or "I Love New York" (which has spawned an industry of copied promotions). I often think Mel Brooks nailed this subject on the head in his movie *Meatballs*. In a scene discussing how the movie they are making can be merchandised before its even made, Brooks unveils a table filled with samples of merchandising products such as Meatballs: the Sweatshirt; Meatballs: the Towel; and Meatballs: the Toilet Paper. They will guarantee the movie's success. Unfortunately, he didn't think of including a Meatballs Pavilion at a Meatballs Theme Park, or, in '90s style, a Fifth Avenue mega-store.

Theme parks and the expansion of this entertainment related environment into restaurants, fast food chains, and shopping malls have developed a further outreach of the licensing program into the creation of a total fantasy environment. The surroundings are a complete escapist world in which the consumer is offered experiences that foster the desire to buy some object in order to retain the memory of the experiences. It's fun, expensive, and big business. These enterprises are a source of employment to graphic and industrial designers as well as architects, illustrators, and planners. Every facet of these parks require graphics, products, and environmental design. The Disney Imagineering group is famous for developing this work genre, but there are several others.

Theme Parks

The phenomenon of licensing promotion exploded in the 1980s and has produced an expanding industry, mainly catering to team sports and cartoon characters. Licensing can also include fashion designers lending their names to fragrances and accessories. In fact, any famous personage, brand, city, country, or entertainment vehicle is ripe for exploration or exploitation, depending upon your viewpoint. Nonetheless, all these products and their accompanying logos need to be designed, and so offer interesting avenues of employment. The significant factor in all this activity is the growing demand for a sophisticated product. Quality of design is an integral part of much that is produced. The graphic designer's input and imagination has moved this industry to the higher ground.

Image Branding

The branding of these images is the motivating strategy, so that Mickey Mouse, The Muppets, Peanuts, and NFL (National Football League) teams, to name a few, are becoming marketable brands. The branding phenomenon moves the images or characters far beyond their sometimes humble origins. Branding produces a perception in the consumer that they are "buying into" the essence of what the character represents. The branding function creates products and merchandising systems every bit as sophisticated as those used in merchandising a designer fragrance. The image (i.e., design) of the product must be appropriate to the marketplace. Accessories, home furnishings, and clothing are sold to all age and economic groups. The 1990 Disney Consumer Product catalogue included over 14 thousand items, in these categories: apparel and toys (the two largest categories), home furnishings, paper goods (including greeting cards and stationery), and gifts and collectibles. They can be found in mass market and upscale retailers, such as K-Mart or Bloomingdales, as well as retail outlets devoted just to the brand itself (the store becomes an environmental design project). A watch can cost $12.95 or thousands of dollars.

Corporate Licensing

Licensing has also expanded to the corporations, who are applying their image to incentive or consumer products, in a desire to proliferate the branding of their corporate identity. It is an interesting mixture of image and marketing when catalogues offer company logos affixed to mugs, jewelry, luggage, etc. Apple computers, Aetna Insurance, and American Airlines offer a broad range of products to consumers and employees. The inherent, differing natures of these corporations also offer insight as to how divergent the corporate image can be and still adapt itself to this marketing arena.

It is important to be observant and to analyze all that you see as a member of our society. Consider what development and design is behind these products the next time you see them on the marketplace. Remember their purpose and that graphic designers are employed for the creation of the design impact. ■

7

Industrial Design

This survey of industrial design (ID) is directed toward its relationship to graphic design. While industrial design is a discipline unto itself, no discussion of graphic design would be complete without considering the alliance of the two.

ID: A Cornerstone in the Evolution of Graphic Design

The origin of industrial design in the 1920s has been glamorized by larger than life figures who gained much media attention. Raymond Lowey, Donald Deskey, and Henry Dreyfuss were true renaissance men who integrated many facets of two-dimensional and three-dimensional design. Lowey, somewhat like Frank Lloyd Wright, was famous for his personal charisma, his vision of design's role in our culture, and his ability to attempt any kind of project. His fame defined the classical American designer. He was responsible for the design of locomotives, automobiles (the Studebaker), corporate identity (Exxon), packaging (Lucky Strike cigarettes), housewares, and china dishes. Lowey's designs had a profound effect in shaping the look of modern-day life in the middle of this century. Industrial design took on an aura similar to architecture (often called the mother of all the arts) and certainly was instrumental in moving the idea of graphic design forward as a profession.

Current ID Practices

Today ID has developed into a business dominated by small scale design firms that can still control an unusual array of diversified assignments. While ID's focus is primarily three-dimensional as opposed to graphic design's two-dimensional base, the industrial designer can still have a significant graphic involvement. Sometimes the firm or individual will do it all, or sometimes opt to work in tandem with graphic designers.

In fact, ID most often encompasses product design and product development. The graphic component is utilized in relation to the product and is often applied graphics. Product development can, because of its intrinsic nature, require or spin off into full-blown identity programs. The products naturally can be anything and everything consumers use, from disposable to durable products. This includes the design (but not engineering) of transportation vehicles (cars, planes, bikes, motorcycles); consumer products (bottles, jars, containers); durable and "white" products (refrigerators, coffee makers, small electrical equipment, household products, eyeglasses, etc.); scientific equipment and instruments (computers, medical and surgical products, instrumentation panels, testing devices); housewares and tabletop (dishes and giftware, cookware, eating utensils); and furniture.

All design work of this nature relies heavily on training and the ability to understand human factors (the guidelines for products being used by the human body, the ergonomic requirements of a product that is reflective of human needs, as pioneered by Henry Dreyfuss) and the designer's proactive role in research and development. Industrial designers are often charged by their clients with the developmental problem-solving required to establish a new product, or they may initiate and create new product ideas based on their own observations. The R & D (research and development) aspect to ID is truly innovative design not experienced in many other design disciplines.

The applied graphics on ID projects are an inherent part

of the complete design program. Often the industrial designer will create all the two- and three-dimensional design. The two-dimensional components of three-dimensional projects are most often realized in identifying or decorative graphics, signage, and exhibition design. It is common practice for industrial design or exhibition design firms to hire graphic designers to work as part of the design team or form co-op ventures with graphic design firms.

A survey of industrial design projects which would incorporate graphic design would include the following:

Product Design

Products frequently need graphics. Sometimes graphics are instructional or informational. Sometimes they are purely decorative. Computers and medical or telecommunications instruments require labels, numbers, buttons, instructions, and general typographic information. Sporting equipment, clothing, and accessories have become graphically decorative. For example, consider the aerodynamic graphics on the clothing used by teams in the 1996 Olympics. This purely graphic impact contributed an altogether new dimension to the visual impression of the sporting event. And the revolution started by Swatch in watch design challenged a whole industry to seek new graphic dimensions for product design. Often when these graphic solutions unite with the name of the product, we enter the world of licensing as well (i.e., Nike sneakers, Head skis, NFL clothing and accessories, Mickey Mouse watches).

Environmental Design / Exhibition Design

Retail environments, public spaces, trade shows, museums, special exhibitions, and corporate shows are the venue for this work. The three-dimensional planning and graphics cannot be separated. The graphics in exhibitions often require an editorial feel or point of view, for they tell a story. Museums devoted to history encompass time lines (Ellis Island, The Rock & Roll Museum, The Johnstown Flood, for example). (See chapter 5, Environmental Design.)

Multimedia / Audio Visuals

Within this genre of work lies the input of the A/V specialist. In the past, slide projectors were routinely utilized to help tell the story. Today our technology allows for more sophisticated solutions. Interactive video is the most popular new technology with virtual reality representing the next break-through medium. Interactive video empowers the observer to play a proactive role in choosing paths and directions of exploration. For example, an exhibition will show a demonstration of Pompeian architecture by allowing the viewer to look at floor plans of a building, then make selections on touch-sensitive video screens as to which rooms to visit and which walls in those rooms to view. By pressing selections, you can move through the house, observing and learning the history of various artworks at your own pace, concentrating on individual points of interest. Computers can now be spoken to as well as touched (keyboard or on screen) to signal the viewer's wishes.

Virtual reality will accelerate the viewer's participatory role. In VR the participant dons a helmet or goggles that encompasses the total visual experience, blocking out any "real world" peripheral vision. The individual is visually submerged into an artificial landscape. A glove is fitted with micro processors that permit the viewer to point his or her way though the territory screened on the goggles. Voice activation is soon to be developed. Thus the viewer controls the choices and moves through the artificial environment as a participant. Applications of VR exist in training programs for the military, programs that simulate flight or combat, and in architectural or engineering programs which allow a type of immersion into a CAD system. Its future in graphic design applications has yet to be determined.

In each of these multimedia examples the dynamic of the process is changing, making the participant a proactive part of the "exhibition" instead of a passive observer.

A/V work has also meant business meetings, conventions, and conferences. These meetings and seminars can be relatively small affairs, requiring simple charts and graphs, or extremely elaborate "special events" utilizing sophisticated technical projections, music (sometimes original), theatrical lighting, stage sets, and state-of-the-art stage craft. At this point these meetings become industrial shows, which are famous for presenting all the talent that money can buy. Entertainment personalities from TV, movies, or the stage are found participating with choreographers, composers, and directors of equal talent. It's a form of pure "show biz" and graphic designers have learned to function within this realm.

Special events can also include many of the same talents listed above devoted to some charitable event. Corporations sponsor fund raisers and utilize their in-house design staff to provide the invitations, menus, banners, decorations, and any other graphic component needed.

Signage

The development of sign systems found in airports, shopping malls, hospitals, office buildings, zoos, mass transportation, and the like require a special group of skills. (This subject correlates to the work of environmental designers; see chapter 5.) The designer needs to be highly organized with a strong ability to analyze and structure information while having a love for and commitment to typographic and graphic systems (graphic design). The designer also needs to know manufacturing materials and three-dimensional structural elements (usually stemming from an ID education). Lastly, the designer has to be able to draw and read drafting plans (architectural drawings). The need for these unique skill combinations explains why signage designers can, and do, develop from all three disciplines.

Signage designers are a special folk who derive much pleasure from their ability to work within a fully integrated design environment. These projects, by their nature, require the collaboration of architects, store planners, industrial designers, and graphic designers. It is an interesting milieu.

The Graphic Design Connection

To recap this short survey of industrial design, I should point out how industrial design functions as an occupation with inter-connecting bonds to graphic design. The relationship between the two disciplines has had several developments beneficial to graphic design. Initially, ID pointed the way for graphic design to be recognized as a discipline unto itself. The development of ID as a profession has also pro-vided a guide and model toward establishing graphic design as a recognized profession. However, at this writing, graphic design has not achieved that status. It is a complex question of accreditation and licensing. Architects must be licensed by the state in which they practice. Industrial designers are not licensed, but through their membership in the Industrial Design Society of America, attach "IDSA" after their name, much the way architects will attach "AIA" (The American Institute of Architects) after their names. This signifier denotes a level of professional acceptance and elevates the individual in the public and clients' eyes. Graphic design has no equivalent practice.

In presenting the alliance between these two disciplines it is interesting to observe how these design careers can merge. Quite often industrial designers find their life's work ends up being graphic design. Some of the motivating forces are the sheer quantity of graphic design projects available compared to the much smaller industrial design business arena. While ID represents an important, integral discipline in the large scope of design, there are fewer industrial designers, fewer firms and, naturally, fewer positions. And, of course, the transition from ID work to graphic design is fairly simple because of the breadth of ID education. It is harder for the graphic designer to function as an industrial designer. To do so usually requires an intense involvement with design in the third dimension or enrolling in an ID program. ■

8

Digital and Interactive Design

The original edition of this book was written in 1992 and the opening of this chapter (then entitled "Computer Graphics") stated: "anything written about the latest innovations is obsolete possibly at the time of writing and certainly by the time of publication." As I write this in the later half of 1996 that caveat is still necessary and true. The dilemma for anyone who attempts to provide an overview of what is "current" in this fascinating and complex field, dependent upon the latest technological progresses, is dismaying as the continuous chain of advancements show no sign of slowing. The appropriate response to solving this problem could be to put this book or chapter online where it could be continuously up-dated, thus eliminating the need to publish on paper obsolete or dated information. However, there are many comforts and practicalities to published material, and information in this format has great value. This is an excellent example of some alternatives and options for delivering information, each with its own value in terms of longevity and relevance. It is obvious that the impact of technology has permanently changed the workplace within a very few years. We believe that the basic methods of operation in graphic design firms have stabilized and the future seems a question of upgrading of tools, always meaning more power, more storage capacity, and ease and speed in operation. We also know that the technical momentum is toward a shift to new media. Of course, online methods of delivery, as well as the upgrading of graphic capability and sophistication have a considerable way to go. Much of what is currently offered on Web sites (with great pride and awe) is problematic. But the possibilities of the future of new media are already in sight. The static quality of graphics are being alleviated through animation and video. Downloading images becomes faster daily with the advent of faster processors and modems. And, the inevitability of the broadening of bandwidth from telephone lines to cable ensures further speed. Through RealAudio and similar technologies, sound is becoming as integral a component on the Web as motion. CD-ROMs and higher density tape and disk drives (e.g., Syquests, Zip, and the like) will change, offering greater capacity and adaptability. Virtual Reality technology has become more than a plaything and the challenge is in usage and applications ahead. I can only believe that in a few years we will look back at the current offerings as rudimentary and crudely presented.

The speed of change challenges everyone's imagination, as well as her energy and dexterity in keeping abreast of the innovations. Nonetheless, while the technology must always be monitored with a watchful eye, we now have enough perspective to view its impact with some clarity.

A Short History of a Short History

The utilization of computers in design firms began shortly after the Macintosh and the PC were introduced in the early 1980s. In 1985 computerized multimedia was limited to on-screen PowerPoint-style slide shows, with bulleted text on a small range of colored backgrounds, but no sound and no video. More often, the term multi-media still meant on-screen video with a separate, but complementary, sound track and lighting. Hypertext allowed for the first interactive computer experience, enabling the user to jump from a reference in one document to related references located elsewhere. In the early 1990s, interactive digital technologies fully emerged, allowing for touch screen kiosks and consumer titles on CD-ROMs. By 1994 Mosaic added graphic capabilities to the Internet, paving the way for uses with more mass appeal and the explosion of the World Wide Web. In the last year, businesses of all types have integrated the Web into their strategies and new uses emerge daily.

The introduction of such digital and interactive technologies with significant graphics capabilities has rapidly attracted the attention of design firms and brought graphic designers to the attention of a multitude of industries. But it has also caused alternating confusion, acceptance, and denial. Many companies have experienced periods of difficult decision-making to justify the expense of this innovation, determine whether it was even necessary, or identify the appropriate equipment to purchase. Many costly investments were made in hardware that today are completely obsolete. Our experience with the computerized design environment is so brief in time and so profound in scope that the challenge of how the individual will dominate the machine is, in some circles, still a topic of major concern. We obviously must be creatively dominant, but many echo the fear that the seduction of instant gratification is changing the way we think and design—but not for the better. As we shall see, traditional skills have not been lost and need to be retained.

Computers have become the indispensable tool; a presence moving from the single unit at a shared table to their ubiquitous presence at each designer's desk, connected by sometimes extensive networks. The drop in initial costs (as with most new electronic equipment) has greatly contributed to this proliferation. At this point a fully equipped studio with individual access to current technology is the standard.

During the mid to late 1980s our requests for hiring would sometimes note that computer experience was a plus factor in the decision making process. In other words, if a designer had some Macintosh literacy they were way ahead of the pack and most often knew more than the person doing the hiring. By 1990 the tables had completely turned, with Mac literacy more often than not a necessity. Today the requirements of digital fluency are standard, with small variations of software proficiency as the deciding factor. Another aspect in this transformation is that young designers will not take jobs with firms that are not technologically current. These designers feel that lack of access to up-to-date equipment will limit their creativity and hamper their careers in the long term. And they are right! Therefore, many of the questions raised in the past regarding technology's viability in design are long dead and buried. The creative studio is electronic, interactive, and online. The on-going challenge is to obtain, maintain, and purchase the most innovative equipment available, for this is the dominant technological force in graphic, architectural, and product design studios.

Today's Workplace

While the importance of computer proficiency is a foremost consideration—and we shall discuss the differing functions where computer design is pertinent—we should not lose sight of its role as a tool. One of my clients stated the issue well, remarking that he wanted designers who were "computer-proficient" but not "computer-dependent." Currently available software is very seductive, and will only become more so. Nonetheless, designers must resist allowing their creative choices to be swayed by their ability to achieve instant gratification or visual and typographic "tricks" or "eye-candy." Designers must rely on all their skills and all the available tools.

Much to the surprise of many designers immersed in the digital revolution, hand drawing continues to be very important. *Drawing remains the base of all visual communication.* It is the point of initial inspiration, as well as the means for demonstrating sensitivity and nuances not duplicated by any other method. Tweaking a type font from a pull-down menu is not acceptable to many of my clients, who are seeking designers who know how to design with type. The computer has not destroyed the importance of drawing, just as mass manufacturing has not destroyed (and may have increased the appreciation of) hand crafts. Colleges have responded by including computer courses as a part of the requisite curriculum without discarding (and in some cases re-initiating) traditional skills such as the letterpress (a fine arts print press process in which paper is selected, type is hand-placed, hand-inked, and run through the press).

In this climate of transition, the paths that firms seek, the roles designers play, and the challenges that need to be met create brain teasers for the best professionals. Everyone is groping and feeling their way through the maze, but since it's such a fast-moving terrain, few have the luxury of time.

The computerized workplace shows other indications of this revolution. The movement toward faster work patterns, with clients expecting project turnaround in an unprecedented short time period has added certain dangers to the field. Some small studios which cannot provide strategic planning as an integral part of the creative process may find themselves so computer-driven that they become a technologically up-to-date version of production houses, providing a commodity, but not a design service. The business climate is ever pushing toward faster and, therefore, cheaper. Since design firms charge clients a service fee based on billable hours, time has become the lynch-pin of cost. As technology allows projects to be completed in shorter periods of time, design firms must find a way to protect themselves and the way the fees are structured. This presents a profound challenge to many companies. Many firms, reversing this trend, have senior level personnel producing the finished work on computer. This is often seen as a waste of creative talent, resented by the designers, but it provides a reason for billing clients at a higher hourly rate. Neither direction produces a satisfactory solution. Tom Weisz, executive vice president of Imergy comments: "Many of today's processes, while using computers, are not helping creative people to work more creatively, but are making creative individuals enslaved to the production process. Creative individuals must strive to change this by becoming more proactive in this communication revolution. Only by helping to shape this new medium will the process favor the creative individual."

Design Solution or Commodity?

Today, the computerized workplace has significantly changed requirements, as a new ability to function through electronically linked sites, modems, and faxes has relaxed the need for workers or companies to be grounded in a specific locale. Firms are decentralizing and so are their employees. Women in particular are benefiting as they can work at home, remaining with their young families, and modem their work to the design firm. Telecommunications innovations and electronic information transfer will probably have a substantial future impact as firms will be able to communicate with their clients, employees, and production output facilities through their computer networks. There are firms in New York online with facilities in the Far East,

Electronic Linkage

connected by satellite or secured online networks, issuing original design information and printing instructions. Design firms establishing satellite offices in other cities can often get much of the work accomplished in the home office.

At this time there seem to be three dominant structural directions for the digital design office. First, the computer has replaced traditional production methodologies and, while graphic designers may be working directly on the computer, their designs are being implemented by more technically oriented computer graphic artists. Second, technology is being utilized for new, innovative creative mediums. Lastly, there is the newly important interactive design component, which has allowed some companies another medium to offer to clients, while others have become immersed in it and have developed a separate profit center or agency. All of these directions represent paths which the traditional graphic designer may explore to seek other tools and creative mediums.

New and Interactive Media

New media generally refers to any product that has an interactive format regardless of the platform used (such as CD-ROM, kiosk, or on-line Web sites and intranet systems). Web sites have proliferated and, while initially the CD-ROM seemed to offer the most promise, today the World Wide Web is clearly the dominant medium. It is this area that has captured the imagination of many designers. Many prefer to work on interactive projects and not traditional design, which has contributed to the enormous talent drain for the classical design firm. Unquestionably the area with the most potential for growth, it still draws heavily from traditional design values and talent. The growth and new opportunities for designers will come not only with the proliferation of Web sites, but also from developing forms of technology, which combine motion and sound. New media requires that designers work in tandem with writers, composers, producers, and programmers, in a structure much like film companies. New skills and forms of communication are needed to produce integrated interactivity. Designers face a new challenge as the new media deliverable requires that meaningful and useful information be married to the visual to engage the viewer and initiate responses. All interactive design demands the re-defining of creative roles and offers numerous design challenges in a medium delineated by the size and definition of a computer or video screen, and subject to the factors of page formats, near-static quality, scrolling, hyperlinks, bandwidth, and speed.

Some Viewpoints by the Pros

I've often observed that if you ask five people for their contemplations on any given topic, you can expect at least six opinions. In an effort to take the temperature of the current climate of thinking and try to get a perspective on what could be coming down the road, I've asked a few people who are in positions to offer good guidance about their thoughts on today and tomorrow. Here are their responses:

Bruce Wands, chair, computer art department, School of Visual Arts, New York stated:

Artists who have expertise in new media are in great demand, especially on the West Coast. The current need is for artists who are well versed in the traditional art disciplines, and also have computer skills. Creativity, originality, and individual style are looked at as the most important qualities. One's portfolio should include examples of computer art as well as drawings, photographs, etc. Sketch books can also give a recruiter insight into your creative potential. As more college graduates become computer literate, the future trend in hiring will be to focus more on creative talent than on software skills.

The following is the closing statement Bruce wrote for the 1996 3D Design Conference. While it is specific to animation, it says it for all career paths.

To have a dream is inspiring, to achieve it is gratifying. There are many ways to enter the 3D animation industry. First and foremost should be your enjoyment of the creative process. Once committed, it is only a matter of time before you will work in the industry. Hard work, being a team player, and creative talent are the main ingredients in becoming a successful 3D animator. A strong foundation in the arts, with a good working knowledge of the hardware and software, are the building blocks of this type of career.

Kenneth Cooke, executive vice president and worldwide creative director of Siegel & Gale talked about the relationship between technology and design:

Technology allows a designer to design, create, and manipulate images, edit or write copy, and set type exactly the way they want it. But this enhanced capability also carries certain demands. Now a designer must not only have an understanding of design history and how different design approaches to a given problem may be more appropriate than others, but also have a critical and discerning eye for illustration and photography (and the ability to alter it if need be). Ideally, they should have professional writing skills and know how to finesse typography. And multimedia puts even more demands on the designer, because now the content can be accessed randomly, images move and may include sound. And while technology allows individual designers to create virtually anything they can imagine, technology can't create content. And content should drive everything.

Steve Dolbow, executive vice president of Siegel & Gale's interactive media division, offers the following from his perspective on career development for new media, which he calls "Looking Forward":

Interactive media positions began to appear, in the middle '80s, when computer companies introduced "multimedia" as a tool for more exciting presentations and games. Later, commercial online services and the World Wide Web brought "multimedia" to life, fueling a new generation of computer users, expecting exciting colors, animations, sound, and lights, and other MTV like elements. This ability for the computer to "speak" to users in the user's language, when the user wants, has drastically increased the demand for information. As a result of this new demand, new business opportunities in communications led traditional communication professionals to embrace the computer as a communication medium.

Today, we see a whole new breed of communications professionals, ranging from the business strategists who create the concepts for the new media to the authors and computer operators who make the computers "dance." Each profession in the chain eventually "morphed" [in digital parlance, morphing is a process that allows a visual shift from one image to another] to a different dimension with new skills and new knowledge required for success.

The challenge is to anticipate the skills and knowledge that will be required in the future as this trend progresses and the rate of the change accelerates. This brief history, while only the beginning, gives us a look into the future at the fundamental forces which are driving this wave of change.

Look at the trends in interactive media. In the past computers spoke to us, on their schedule, with reports, documents, and "green screens." Today we see moving images, hear words and music, and get access to services, all on our schedules. This is a part of the "anytime, anywhere" promise of senior computer company executives in the early '90s. A promise which is now beginning to be delivered.

The most significant force for change in the interactive media is the growing ability of the computer to be "human centric." This change has spawned a need for programmers with a sense of design, designers with a knowledge of technology, artists who embrace digital canvasses, and given creative professionals new tools to build brands and sell products. So what does this tell us about the future?

The creative communicators of the future will need to work even harder staying up with the changes in technology. Each platform is developing its own language, unique capabilities, and skill requirements. The client reps, project managers, and producers need to understand these changes and create programs of communications that take advantage of the technology, without being led by it. This is a difficult balance, but absolutely necessary.

The designers and artists who succeed will understand the power of, and know how to harness, the third dimension that this media brings to life. As new technologies, such as voice recognition, intelligent agents, ubiquitous bandwidth, and others come along, we must welcome them and learn how they can facilitate the age old challenge of communicating an idea from one mind to another. Experience in dealing with moving images or music will be a tremendous asset. An excitement for learning is mandatory. Fear of change will be deadly.

Systems managers and programmers are a new addition to the interactive media team. Interactive media solutions require team members who can talk to the MIS staff, perform technology surveys, do systems audits, create industrial strength systems solutions, connect databases to servers and clients, and more. The exact technology skills vary from project to project however, each professional needs to be dedicated to learning specific technologies. Overall, they need to focus on cognitive psychology, interface design, usability testing, and other skills that will help them create user centric applications.

Red Burns, chair, New York University Interactive Telecommunications Program, added:

> I think the most essential criterion is intelligence—an ability to understand what the graphic design is trying to convey. I don't believe it is about pretty pictures; I believe the field is about designing information which requires acute intelligence.

A Guide to Jobs in Digital Design
by Rita Armstrong

Rita Armstrong heads my firm's digital and interactive design department. She responds to the daily business demands for technically oriented creative talent in print production and interactive media. Rita advises our candidates on options, positioning, and career directions. She can offer the reader important, first-hand knowledge concerning career directions, as well as the pit-falls facing the job-seeker. Most importantly, she addresses the issues of graphic design versus digital design choices in a career path. Rita also advises clients as to how to structure their firms to integrate personnel into existing departments or how to develop these departments into separate profit centers. Her expertise is especially relevant now that new media has created opportunities for growth for both individuals and companies. I've asked for her perspective on jobs and technology because she has witnessed the failures and successes. Here is her analysis of the current placement climate to help those seeking directions in what often seems an uncharted maze.

THE DILEMMA

The designer must ask, "What am I, a designer with killer computer skills and cyber talent, or am I a production artist with the ability to flesh out others' designs and be innovative with type?"

Answering this question honestly may be one of the toughest assignments a person may ever have. The answer will affect your career from its roots to its finale. However, the job applicant isn't the only one faced with this quandary. The employer sits staring blankly at job descriptions and questions his or her need for a designer gifted with technical know-how or a computer-head with some design capabilities.

Over the years, this dilemma has become more complicated. The use of Photoshop collage images and computer illustrations has blossomed with the growth of new media. Are these artists, designers, or computer production specialists? The truth is, they are neither, but something somewhere in between. The real issue for the designer is deciding what he/she wants to be, and finding an employer who feels the same way about that role in their design process. It is also the best issue to confront when filling a position. If the employer finds him- or herself sitting across the desk from someone whose eyes light up every time the company's approach to the design process is discussed, he or she should hire that interviewee. That person is already considering how he or she can serve that process.

Mac and PC artists as well as digital designers should know that titles have become meaningless in their field. I know an art director who is paid around 45 thousand dollars to be a production artist with a type sense. I also know computer artists who should have design titles, because the balance of their work is conceptual. Interactive designers rely heavily on the artistic sense of their programmers and production artists. The lines drawn between the design process and production implementation are becoming even more vague.

The dilemma offers a variety of minefields and blessings. When the designer is considering his or her role in print and technology, he or she should know that there are ways to utilize technical skills to reach a design goal. If overseeing a computer network and getting occasional design projects is a goal, understand that 50 to 70 percent of the time will be used servicing other designers' technical needs. If a person doesn't have a strong enough portfolio to be hired for design only, this option allows for a method of portfolio development while earning a living.

After the decision is made as to career direction, the designer needs to package him- or herself as such. When going on an interview or even designing a résumé, take note of how computer experience is stressed. Is it listed at the top of the résumé? How much is software management mentioned or used in the body copy? Are technical skills up to date? If involved in Web site design, are the most recent URLs (that is, Universal Resource Locators or Web site addresses) listed, or will the prospective employer be looking at sites that are outdated or that no longer represent the designer's work? Too many designers fail to list URLs and their technical knowledge properly. It shows a lack of marketing savvy.

If, after all the soul searching, packaging, and interviewing, the person finds they are failing to be called back for second interviews, it is time to retool. It maybe time to reconsider which talents are strongest and where they are most appropriate. If computer skills are good and the designer is failing to be called back for design positions, it is time to realize that design may not be that person's calling. Technical production jobs in both print and interactive are not without glory, especially if Photoshop and Illustrator skills are sharp. There is a lot of career gratification to be found as a respected part of the team, and salaries are often at least as high as designers'.

WHAT ARE YOU WALKING INTO?

In the glorious realm of technology there are no guarantees. (As though other creative areas could so generously offer such an intangible prize.) Now that a large portion of my work includes placement in new media, I can vouch for the surreal vanity of start-up companies with job description promises. Get a job description in writing if possible. Are they asking for a programmer, a designer, or a technical lead? Employers don't always know and therefore it's important to ask what is expected. The person doing the hiring may think Quark has something to do with Physics 101 and nothing more, or that a complicated Photoshop file can be delivered in an hour.

Writing a clear, concise job description may be a painful, but necessary, process for employers. It allows them to take stock of what skills are necessary and in what order of importance. Too many employers interview candidates with the idea that they will "know it when I see it." This leaves too much left unsaid at interviews and allows the employer to get away with not addressing the negatives. The interview becomes an audition and the candidate is left without any solid ideas of what is expected of them.

If the person is a techie, the job description should include what hardware and software are to be utilized. This information will reveal how much knowledge the department head has about the specialty. Job applicants have a right to question whether the budget includes conferences and tutorials. Before taking a job, whether it be a print position or a Web designer spot, it's important to know that the new company is committed to the technology. I remember one candidate included the fee for Mac Expo as a part of a sign-on package. This let him know whether the company that wanted to hire him was also interested in supporting the technology during his employment. They informed him that they could only send one person and, while he might be the logical choice, the vice president usually went. He turned down the position.

WHAT'S HOT AND WHAT'S NOT

New media has created a whole host of hot job descriptions: new media technical animation directors, creative managers, designers, producers, account and production staff. I see a general need for designers who know the capabilities and limitations of the medium. Creative managers need to have a strong technical knowledge in order to understand deadline expectations and how appropriate those expectations are. One of the better creative managers I know has taken programming classes at NYU. It allows her the freedom to assign realistic schedules to her technical staff. They respect her knowledge of their expertise and therefore perform better. Consequently, she is compensated for her knowledge. She earns approximately 120 thousand dollars plus valuable stock in the company. Web designers need to know some HTML. They won't be required to use it all that often (unless they freelance) but they need to know how to design around its limitations.

I truly enjoy working with illustrators and Photoshop artists who have brought their talent into the cyber age. If a designer has a flair for sharp images with contrast and punch, he or she should consider multimedia. Not long ago, an advertising director called me to find some strong icon and Photoshop designers because he felt his firm's online work looked stagnant. I surfed to their Web site and had to agree. It looked like a crude collection of stock photos, with decent type and good programming. Photoshop experts and computer illustrators could turn their site into something energetic and fresh. These production/design positions are usually listed at salaries of 35 to 60 thousand dollars and also provide a lot of freelance employment.

Requests for the interactive hybrid are increasing. These positions are for those left brain/right brain people who seem to know all the answers on "Jeopardy." They can manage Internet sites with technical and conceptual input. The titles vary. I placed someone with these skills under the title "Junior Webmaster." His total compensation package was about 45 thousand dollars.

Demand for gaming expertise in both design and pro-gramming will grow stronger, as Web technology becomes more sophisticated. Advertisers recognize this as an opportu-nity to market entertainment while selling their product. Good story board artists are hard to find. They support the sales and development of gaming CD-ROMs and Web sites. Salaries vary, but are rather impressive in this area.

Believe it or not, print is alive and kicking. Corporate identity computer production artists top the list in areas of active recruitment. Producing corporate identity manuals may not seem sexy, but it pays well (anywhere from 35 to 65 thousand dollars, depending on level of expertise). Corporate communication firms also offer humane work environments and in most cases, steady, reasonable hours.

In addition, cross-platform knowledge for both print and interactive is a very marketable. Positions can be difficult to fill because they require extensive PC import knowledge. These appear most often under the title of production man-agement, especially for corporations and catalog companies.

Salaries range from 45 to 80 thousand dollars, depending on the number of staff.

Advertising agencies constantly need junior Mac artists. Some of these positions offer growth in conceptual input and others are strictly production oriented. Be cautious as the titles rarely reflect the job content. Freelance before accepting a staff position, if possible. These positions usually offer about 30 thousand dollars a year.

The areas that currently seem to be at an employment standstill are CD-ROM design and high-level advertising production spots. Salaries for computer production have leveled off because technical expertise is a requirement for hiring, not an added bonus. Those who do not have intermediate to expert level skills in at least three programs are finding few opportunities. I would advise them to increase their competence with an updated educational program and find freelance work to put in their books. It would make sense to learn several interactive applications as well. As new media becomes ubiquitous in usage, it will expand the demands in development. This will not so much create new jobs, but change the expectations in software knowledge for existing positions, as small companies gain interactive assignments from present print clients.

TECHNOLOGY AND PORTFOLIO PRESENTATION

So, whether one is a print or interactive designer, flexing those multimedia muscles by putting work in an interactive format may seem like a terrific idea. In most cases it is not the best way to present a portfolio.

Stating it simply, interactive résumés are a pain and are not worth the time unless they reveal more than a paper résumé can. They make the prospective employer work too hard in order to know the basics. Who wants to hire anyone whose first impression is that they don't understand how busy most people are, or perhaps don't value time? Out of the hundreds of interactive formats I've received, only one CD stands out as a marketable tool for representation. And even that piece had to be retooled because the first edition had a glitch.

Retooled, the second CD worked well, so well that I was able to set up five interviews in a week after circulating the piece. The interface was simple. It divided the job seeker's experience by sample work, technical knowledge, and employers. By simply clicking samples, the pieces appear with a description of where, how, and why they were produced. He also included inactive Web pages, as well as print projects. This method of showing samples is expensive and time-consuming and perhaps should only be considered by those who are relocating and do not have produced URLs or a personal URL to view.

Show screen grabs if they appear sharp enough. If you are fortunate enough to have been published, include a color copy of the article with your résumé and in your book, especially if it features photos of your work. Call and check before you drop off a 270 Syquest or Zip. You may be screened by a human resources specialist first and he or she won't have the equipment to view your work. Part of marketing yourself is knowing your audience and catering to their needs. It also means respecting them until they have proven that respect is undeserved. Show your technical talent in an accessible manner and you will make a long lasting impression that just may get you the job you've always wanted . . . The computer is the tool. The master is the one who uses it to reflect the depth of his or her talent.

Combining Talents and Teams in Interactive Media by Jessica Eve Goldfarb

As we have observed, all creative businesses are driven by a combination of talents; creative, strategic planning, marketing, and business development. Interactive media is no different and therefore I have asked Jessica Goldfarb to provide an over-view of the individual roles and skills required to produce the final product.

Surely, 1994 to 1996 will go down in history as the period during which the Internet and interactive media exploded in the American awareness and lexicon, as well as a serious form of business. At the start of that short period, the World Wide Web did not even exist; by its end, it has become a ubiquitous feature of nearly all corporate communications from print ads, movie posters, and music CD inserts, to financial documents. As the hot field today, it draws many people, regardless of their work experience.

A BRAND NEW MEDIA

Design, in its commercial context, has always operated in conjunction with business or marketing goals, requiring the involvement of managers and marketers. Interactive design, of course, requires these same functions. In particular, savvy businesses have discovered the power of interactive media to convey information and experiences to extend a brand's equity or to help businesses to operate more effectively. The mcrc fact that information is delivered interactively enhances the audience's retention rate, making the message richer. And, the fact that the medium has made possible real-time, two-way communications, has given businesses invaluable insight into customers and methods to service them. Accordingly, marketing and strategy are key elements to all commercial uses of interactive media.

Good marketers and strategists, therefore, are needed by all interactive media developers, whether at advertising agencies, design firms, production shops, or at in-house corporate divisions. The crucial skill is the ability to truly understand the capabilities and limitations of the media and, therefore, of the technology. Often a cursory understanding of the boundaries is sufficient, but frequently this means getting fairly hands-on. In this new media, more savvy developers have searched long and hard for strategists with extremely detailed understanding to push the known boundaries and fully utilize its potential. Some marketers have begun taking technical courses. Some schools have begun to help strategists think more "outside the box."

As a consequence, companies are always looking for the best strategic talent they can find. No doubt, it will be some time until this field shakes down into anything that resembles standard requirements.

TEAM BUILDING (RAH! RAH!)

Managers in interactive media face this same challenge—having to combine business and technical knowledge. In addition, they often need to have a solid feel for the creative and more specific production skills.

Regardless of the specific organizational structure, interactive media is always created in teams, usually numbering only a few per project. Most teams work in an integrated manner, so each role engages with all others to some extent. This keeps the required knowledge base wide and makes it necessary to "play well with others." The designated team organizer (usually the producer or project manager) will find leadership skills vital to getting the job done. Being able to inspire and establish camaraderie go far in this field. Of course, keen organizational skills come in handy as well.

WE DON'T NEED NO STINKIN' JOB TITLES!

Most often, the organizational structure in interactive shops is roughly akin to film production, with junior or line producers reporting to executive producers and creative or art directors, overseeing the design of the project. But, as Rita noted, no one yet has determined what a producer is; the term varies with each company with regard to how technical, hands-on, and creative the person must be. Some companies use the title project manager instead, and these positions are often identical.

Differences depend in large part on the company's original focus. Advertising agencies have often kept that industry's traditional account/creative division. Design firms frequently use project managers. Even those positions within in-house divisions, which are not directly production related, require that producers or project managers have significant production knowledge, so as to oversee outside shops. Media companies sometimes have completely mixed job titles which are standard in other industries, occasionally having producers report directly to an executive-level editor. Recently, the trend has been toward establishing producers, who are production related, and project managers, who are more account related; but there is much leeway even within this structure.

As Rita also noted, the demand is increasingly for hybrid talent, who are equally right- and left-brained. Companies are of two structures: many are striving toward creative, distinct functions, while others prefer a fluid creative environment. So, when interviewing in this new field of interactive media, it is of utmost importance to be sure to get as much detail as possible about the specific divisions of labor within the company, as well as the expected responsibilities of the particular job. It is better to ask questions to be clear about the job, rather than be surprised later.

PUTTING YOUR BEST FOOT FORWARD

While this field is still young, many people can still easily transition into it from any number of other industries by focusing on their core talents. However, already many companies—especially in the interactive centers of Silicon Alley (NYC) or Multimedia Gulch (San Francisco)—will not even look twice at applicants without hands-on experience in interactive production.

It is always preferable to put any interactive experience on a résumé, listing URLs where applicable. The lack of uniformity makes it necessary to give some description of the contribution to a particular project. Those without significant experience may be wise to seek out courses on these subjects. Most of all, it is best to be clear about skill strengths and career objectives.

A Perspective for Now and the Future

As stated, while the changes and challenges of new media can be difficult to comprehend in such a short time span, the sign posts are now deeply embedded, although the trans–figuration of design continues.

Tom Weisz's comments from 1992 are still true today:

Today's graphic designer or communication professional has the opportunity of a lifetime if they recognize their process is likely to change and they are adaptable to that change. We are at the door to a whole new world in communication. New challenges are emerging and change is the most difficult thing to ask of anyone.

The designer of our time is faced with immense pressure. Each creative individual has an enormous task at hand trying to work within this challenging new world. The creative field needs to look at itself and develop new methods that are beneficial to creative processes and procedures.

While the future may still be foggy, certain truths are evident. Technology is being harnessed by commercial enterprises and the designer must establish his or her role as the arbiter of design and taste for new media. The seductive nature of software will have to become secondary to the creative thought process, only there to provide a wonderful freedom. The shifting responsibilities in the workplace, as well as its very structure, may at times seem confusing, but after all, change always has existed as a function of life. It is a fabulous time to be creative.

I have no doubt that the creative mind will always triumph. Our creativity produced these technologies in the first place. *The machines are only the result of our intellect and surely are no match for our minds.* ■

Getting Started: How Do You Get There?

Starting a job search can be a daunting and sometimes intimidating process. It should be comforting for the novice to know that the experienced professional faces the same challenges and, while for the seasoned designer the ground rules may be familiar, the process is rarely a comfortable one.

Although few people enjoy a job search, the guidelines in this book will point the way not only to a goal but also to a process in which the collateral benefits are educational, informative, and enriching.

Seeking a job or changing jobs means embarking on a process of introspection and exploration. You need to define priorities and goals as well as research opportunities to learn "what's out there." Done properly, such a search gives you an opportunity to study market conditions, take the temperature of firms, and learn more about what's current. It also gives you the chance to interview, allowing entree to the inside of firms not otherwise accessible. How many times do you get a chance to visit competitive companies? Often you only know them by reputation, grapevine gossip, or by seeing work published. And then add to your list the companies referred to you through your networking activities which you never considered. This affords a more objective view of one's

Starting the Search

worth in the marketplace, as well as an evaluation of the marketplace itself.

The ability to go "inside" is all too rare. It affords a very special kind of education to those who are observant. You can learn a lot about the company image as manifested in the

The Work Enviornment

ambiance of the work environment. By just observing the art on the walls, the clothing people wear, their manner of speech, and how you are treated, a comfort level may or may not be established. All this tells you more than any written company profile or job description and ultimately presents the opportunity for eye-to-eye contact, which is the best gauge of all. We will, as often as time permits, visit a client to observe the work environment for all these reasons. Often the tie a man wears, the accessories worn by a woman, the method of communication, the noise level, the existence or lack of interruptions, and the attitude of the receptionist—all send very important messages. These messages are the most telling. They establish the "culture" of the firm and establish the intuitive feelings, which overcome the initial, objective view of a company, making your opinion subjective and attitudinal.

Learning through Exposure

Many times the people I interview request I refer them on as many interviews as possible. This request stems from a sophisticated knowledge of the benefits of interviews. These people are not seeking an easy way out of the job search process. They are not concerned about the time or effort in interviewing, nor are they concerned about exposing themselves to rejection. They want the experience and recognize the advantage of exposure. Unfortunately, I can't send people to my clients without excellent reasons, for that is just what my clients seek our services for—to save them money and the time of unnecessary interviews. However, there are other methods, as we will see, to get an inside peek at the inner workings of companies.

It should be obvious now why a job hunt can be a learning process. The exposure to a variety of personalities, different evaluations, feedback, and critiques, as well as the exposure to the atmosphere of a company, can be an eye opener. It also tells you a great deal about how to make comparisons. The "corporate culture" (an overused term) is evident the minute you walk through the door. This process allows you to form opinions independently, based upon contact and not hearsay.

However, before you get through the door, there is a lot of work to be done. Above all, you want to convince people it is necessary to meet you and you want to make sure you are approaching the right people. You also want the confidence of knowing you are on the best possible trajectory, the best possible strategy for your talent and your goals. *One thing is for sure. You are going to face rejection.* It is a fact of life, so you might as well get used to it. It is a necessary part of the learning process.

Rejection in itself need only be painful if too much emotion is riding on the nature of the contact. Since it is to some degree always inevitable, it's best to recognize it as a fact of life, deal with it, and get on with the rest of your business. So don't let it stop you. You just cannot be all things to all people. Don't let it dim your aspirations or your determination. *Never, never take a rejection as a evidence of your self-worth.* Often the ability to sustain repeated rejection is simply a matter of personal courage—and you'll definitely need a lot of courage. We all do. Too many people I know allow their fear of rejection to influence their decision-making. Sometimes it can stop them cold in their tracks. Sometimes it prevents them from trying the "impossible." Trying—always trying, taking a risk—is one of the most important characteristics for success. Measured risk-taking (not being foolhardy) is a key ingredient in the ability to move forward. So rejection or failure can be the by-product of risk. However, nothing is achieved without risk. In many ways, a certain amount of fear is a healthy, self-regulating emotion—it keeps you on edge and prevents you from becoming "cocky" or, worse, arrogant. Therefore, it's necessary to take a deep breath and "go for it." And, most importantly, keep moving on. Never let setbacks or failures cloud your sight on your goals. I used to work for a firm that had a little neon sign that said "moving right along." I greatly appreciated that message glowing at me in vivid color on days that were black for me. Maybe we all need something like that to keep us moving. However, move you must—or you'll be stopped.

Coping with Rejection

Who Are You?

When presenting yourself to anybody, in a social or business context, the introduction process sends many messages. When embarking on a job search, you need to determine where you want to go and how to introduce yourself into a defined milieu. In order to do that successfully, you must first ask some self-searching questions.

- What am I best at?
- Is what I'm best at what I think I want to do?
- Am I sure about what kind of work I want to do?
- Where do I want to do it?
- Who do I want to do it for?
- What kind of position do I eventually want to hold, or do I want my own firm?

Until you can deal with most of these questions, you're not in a position to accurately introduce yourself to a future employer. It is critical to know yourself and at least your short-term goals in order to make a focused presentation. With self-knowledge you can "package" yourself as an identifiable asset for hire. Our experience has proven that when a person is not clearly focused on their abilities and goals, the message sent to the interviewing individual is confused and the resulting outcome is, at best, indecision. Your goal in any interview or presentation is to present yourself as a clearly focused talent with distinct goals (even if you are not sure and are just testing the water).

So let us go over these key questions that will help establish personal priorities.

Finding Your Creative Focus

1 and 2. What are you best at? Is what you are best at what you think you want to do? What comes easily? Do you sometimes mistrust that which is easily attainable? Do you place too much value on projects that have been a struggle? Is it because you had to sweat over a project that you cannot give it up? I don't want to assume that laboring over a project means it doesn't have value, or has not met with success. It is just that very often we lose our objectivity when our effort becomes labored. Often what comes easily does so because it's more natural to who we are. I remember when I was an undergraduate struggling with the classical empty canvas. I was studying with Robert Motherwell, who was a great influence. I had learned that painting was a metaphor and that the visual poetry was something for which I strived. However, while I loved painting, I had a great deal of trouble painting spontaneously. Everything was such a big decision, so I would stand in front of the canvas—seemingly forever. I painted slowly, although with skill. Ultimately I took a

course in sculpture and found working in three dimensions a snap. But in my mind's eye I considered myself a painter. I didn't take the "sculpture thing" seriously. I mistrusted my natural talents because they were so inherently an extension of myself. I thought it was "healthier" to suffer the angst of creativity.

As a faculty member at Pratt Institute I found students doing the same thing. Perhaps they were intrigued with editorial design. But they really shone in packaging design. Or perhaps there was a fixation with creating logotypes but the person had a natural promotional bent and responded to copy concepts with strong imagery. I'm sure you see the parallels. Think about what it is that you really do best and trust in it—because that is where you will be successful. Uphill battles are not much fun after a while.

3. Are you sure about what kind of work you want to do? Does this question make you particularly nervous? Do you feel something is wrong if you are unsure of yourself and what it is you want to do? You probably feel the ideal is to be totally self-assured with a clear goal in sight and I'm sure you know people who seem to have all the answers. You may find yourself envious of people who seem to be completely in control. For sure, having that clear vision makes it easier. Nonetheless, the majority of both students and people beginning their careers are not sure about what they want to concentrate on. In fact, most people really want to have the most diversified experiences possible. Most designers prefer to be generalists. However, as we have discussed in our survey of graphic design, the marketing or geographical impositions on the field can make it difficult.

So what does this "average" person do? This question leads to the next part of our inquiry:

4 and 5. Where do you want to do it? For whom do you want to do it?

First, you have analyzed what it is that you do best. Now you must research the field. Read all the trade periodicals, see the annuals, study the awards given, learn what work is being done currently and learn who's doing it. Analyze what you see. What do you like? Where does your aesthetic focus seem to lead and what is a logical fit with your philosophical point of view? What companies are on the same critical wavelength as the work you do best?

This is the basic methodology we use with candidates who

Seeking a Path

Where to Work

approach us for work. We look for the visual connections. We try to detect the common threads of an aesthetic approach as exemplified through the presentation portfolio and try to match that to our clients. We think about what would "work" with various firms. For, in the last analysis, when people review portfolios and need to hire, they really want to see what they want to see. Meaning that while they may value and appreciate something other than the way they solve their visual problems, ultimately they will hire because they feel there is a strong relationship between what their firm does and your past experience or what they see in your portfolio. It is the rare person who will hire in order to establish a dramatically different design point of view.

Your Hit List

This is how to start creating the logical links, looking for the connections, and making a "hit list" of companies you'd like to work for. Don't worry if there is some variety in the output of these firms. What is important is that you feel attracted to their output and you feel your own work is compatible. For those working in an area which is dissimilar—for example, you've got a job in a promotional agency, but you want to work on a magazine—an adjustment will have to be made within your portfolio samples. (See chapter 10.) But, for now, know that you are developing a strategy for your future and a methodology for dealing with those goals.

Long-Term Goals

6. What kind of position do you eventually want to hold, or do you want your own firm? This is obviously a question about your long-term goals. However, it is important for you to start thinking about the differences between short-term and long-term goals. So often the short-term pressures become so all-encompassing that anything that smacks of long-term isn't given serious thought. Long-term goals are easily eclipsed by the reality of the daily struggle. Objectivity is lost and the subject doesn't even come up. This question is a memory jogger. You should start thinking about what you may eventually want to do and give serious consideration to the level of responsibility you are comfortable with. Not everyone should be a creative director or president of a firm and take on the responsibility of running a company. Nor should everyone be a freelancer. As you take on jobs and new experiences, look for your role models. Think about what makes you happy. Think about the correlations between title, salary, work hours, and lifestyle, as well as the differences between full-time employment and freelancing.

Networking

Your next step is to develop your personal "hit list" similar to the way I described we work. This will be your target list of companies for whom you would like to work. At this point you should have:

- A sense of what you want to do.
- Researched the firms to which you feel attracted and feel compatible: your "hit-list."
- In other words, you have set priorities and goals. You have your portfolio ready to go (see chapter 10). You are ready.

The first step is to augment your list through personal contacts. If you are a student or a recent graduate, show it to your faculty. Find out who they may know at these firms and if there are other similar firms they might recommend. Go to your placement office and talk it over with a counselor. Think back to summer employment or internship contacts whom you could approach. If you are working, it is time to pull out every business card you have collected to analyze where these people are now and who might be a valuable and interesting contact. If you know people who are printers, paper sales people, or other trades contacts you feel are trustworthy, ask them what they know about hiring opportunities. These service tradespeople are favorite industry couriers of all kinds of information as they travel from firm to firm. They are often asked for referrals by companies who want to hire. They represent a great way to "get the word out."

Portfolio Drop-offs

Start by telephoning the companies on your list. Start at the very top and work your way down. Don't be intimidated by the fame of the firm. The worst that can happen is that you'll be rejected and that is not the worst thing that can happen. We have discussed the relative unimportance of that act. However, who knows, you may be surprised! Ask for the art department or ask who reviews portfolios. Most importantly, you want it to be seen by the right person. Therefore, ask your questions carefully. Find out what their policy is for portfolio review. Most firms will have some kind of structure regarding reviews. It might be on a particular day of the week, or it might be only between certain hours. Ask how long you need to leave your book. *And before you pick it up, make sure it's been seen!* Too often someone may be called out of town or just be busy and not able to see your book. For entry level positions or for people who are not concerned about protecting their confidentiality, the portfolio drop-off is probably the quickest route to get your work seen.

While many people object to the drop-off system as being too impersonal, it has become almost an industry standard, a necessary evil. It is the most direct, time-saving way for a busy, often overworked manager to find the people he or she wants to interview in the first place. You need to remember that while your personality, motivation, and goals are every bit as important as your talent, without the talent the rest isn't necessary. And when someone interviews you, to be even moderately polite, the interviewer must take at least a half an hour. However, it probably takes no more than two minutes at best (and probably much less) to know if a portfolio is interesting. That is a difficult fact for most people to accept, but it's true. The pressure this puts on you to create the best possible portfolio is enormous and we will discuss that in the next chapter. Suffice it to say that the prevalent system caters to our workaholic world, and allows the person who doesn't have a moment to spare the ability to look through portfolios in a flexible period of time, perhaps stolen moments between meetings, and determine whether a book belongs to someone they would want to meet. It is also important for young people to know that this system exists for the very experienced, too. In my firm, on a daily basis, we have to send portfolios first, even when we are submitting people for highly paid positions. I don't want you to think that all job applications are necessarily handled this way. However, the vast majority are.

Developing Contacts

When someone has seen your work, and, hopefully, liked it, they will have some method of letting you know. It may be personally, through an assistant or perhaps a note. What they usually will not tell you is that they didn't like your book. People are always asking for feedback, but they rarely get it, for few want to take the time for a constructive review. The answer most often is a simple "no interest" or "not a fit." Any favorable response should, therefore, be viewed as an opportunity to create a larger network. If they were positive but didn't have an opening, could they possibly recommend other people or firms to you? Most people are really happy to try and help someone, and it is likely one contact may bring you several others. And so it goes on. A domino effect. The true meaning of networking. Don't be timid about asking secretaries, administrative assistants, creative directors, anybody who could help and seems friendly. Don't be shy and feel guilty, as if you are "using" someone. While there are negative implications to people who are indeed "users," these methods are just basic, good business practices.

Diaries for Business Contacts and Taxes

A diary or log of your activities is a necessity at this time. You should keep a record of everyone you contact, the nature of the contact, and, of course, the date. This information can prove to be very important as time moves on. For example, people often change jobs, and the person who indicated an interest in you and didn't have an opening may offer another kind of opportunity for you in another firm. When you are showing your portfolio over a period of many months (yes, it can take many months), it's easy to get confused as to where you've been, or perhaps who asked you to try again in two months. This information also will prove to be an important resource the next time you seek employment.

Did you know there is a tax benefit in conducting a job search? Keeping a complete record of your activities can provide tax deductions on your next return. The key is maintaining a diary or log of everything you do and everybody with whom you have contact.

The IRS is on your side when you are looking for a job within the same field of employment. This means as long as it's a graphic design or advertising position, and you don't want to do something else with your life, the costs incurred in the job search process can be a legitimate tax deduction. You must keep accurate, complete records of all costs applicable to your search. Any expenses directly connected to your work and search, including transportation, lunches, faxes, printing of résumés, even special clothing needed for an interview, and any supplies (thinking of buying a computer?), must be tracked for tax purposes. Besides keeping your diary of portfolio drop-offs and interviews, keep all your receipts by either attaching them to the appropriate diary pages or start a chronological receipt file, separating your costs into travel and entertainment in one category and supplies in another. All costs that exceed 2 percent of your last annual gross earnings can be deducted from the next year's tax return.

Headhunters

Developing a personal affiliation with an excellent head-hunter can result in one of the most important and enduring business relationships. And it's free! It is the recruiter's client (the firm that wants to hire) who pays the recruiter's fee. Our firm only asks the candidate for undying loyalty (and sometimes a thank you) as recognition of our contributions to his or her future. Of course this is the moment when I should proudly proclaim the unquestionably high ethical standards of our work as well as the caliber and quality of my firm. However, putting the self-serving part of it aside, the quality and nature of the relationships we have developed over a period of many years has had a profound affect on many people's lives.

Your headhunter can become your confidant, your career counselor. You can be introduced to opportunities you would never be able to access on your own. When we have been most successful, we have met people whom we have believed in, who have had a talent we could focus on, and therefore introduce to a sector of our client base. We have been able to not only find them a job but track their career over many years and, in some cases, place them in several positions throughout their careers. In other words, we were fundamentally proactive in molding and guiding their careers, finding jobs, business opportunities, and ultimately partnerships, acquisitions, and mergers. These people recognize the value of our relationship, often coming to us for ad hoc career advice or for advice in helping them structure job descriptions and salary/compensation packages with their firms.

The first duty of the professional executive recruiter is to service its client, the firm who wishes to hire, who has asked the recruiter for help to solve a hiring need and who pays the recruiter's fee. The recruiter can only properly refer candidates to the client when the recruiter fully understands the personal capabilities and professional goals of the candidate. So the recruiter walks a fine line between servicing the clients in the best way possible and helping the candidate almost as a "rep," or artist's representative. That is why, so often, our candidates become our clients. And, since we are always on the lookout for new talents, the recruiter can also become a networking resource for the entry-level candidate.

However, it should also be remembered what a recruiter cannot do. A recruiter cannot be your only source, for no one has access to every possibility. And a recruiter cannot be successful for everybody, so recruitment firms may not be able to solve your immediate problems. They may, however, turn out to be an excellent resource the next time around. The best advice is to try to get access to more than one recruiter and see how the relationship develops. The quality of communication between the two of you will determine the quality of your future association.

A Simple "Thank You"

It's a simple maxim: The more successful your networking strategy is, the more expanded your contact list will become. The sheer number of diverse people you'll meet will be an education in itself. You are utilizing many resources: faculty, mentors, friends, business associates, trades people, and executive recruiters (headhunters). And those resources are recommending other contacts. Along the way many people will show an interest in your future and take time from their busy day to avail you of their expertise. It's time then to say a formal thank you with a simple note, and show you not only have good manners but a good business sense. It has often been the finishing cap to an interview for a highly competitive position! I often tell students who have spent a great deal of time and money on their education that the best business move can be achieved for the cost of a stamp. As previously noted, people move around a lot in this business and you never know when you'll meet up with someone again. The platitude, "it's a very round world" is amazingly true! So remember your manners and say "thank you."

Résumés

There are an infinite number of methods to produce a satisfying résumé, and many firms offer professional résumé writing services. I do not recommend résumé services for creative people. My experience has proven that the résumé which accompanies a portfolio has special requirements. Most often this résumé is not viewed by itself, but serves as an companion to a visual presentation. However, when submitted by itself, it must still be able to stand alone, if only as an introduction to the portfolio and/or interview which follows.

The résumé that accompanies a portfolio has to have the following characteristics: It must be clear, concise, clean (no folded corners, creases, or smudges), and without errors. Résumés do not have to be professionally printed, and I am ambivalent about using a résumé to make an unusual design statement. The bottom line is when the design works well, it's great. However, I have seen too many over-designed résumés create a negative impact. Your safest bet is a simple, clearly laid out (that's design), highly legible résumé. Currently, most résumés are typeset on computer. A typewritten résumé is still acceptable but has become a rarity.

The computer has made the possibility of multiple résumés a flexible and easy option. Having more than one résumé is often an excellent idea. One of the most applicable uses would be to change the "objectives" when necessary. It is an appropriate choice for the person who can have different directions to pursue. Just as you can manipulate the structure of your portfolio (see chapter 10, Your Portfolio) you can have two résumés with two separate objectives. For example, you might like to alternately stress your management experience or your creative experience. This could be accomplished by the manner in which your current job responsibilities are emphasized, by focusing on one more than the other.

Dos and Don'ts

Some "do not's" regarding paper choice: Do not use dark-colored paper. It cannot be photocopied. Paper that is too heavy cannot be faxed. For the sake of good taste, do not use pastels that are best left for cosmetic packaging. Some people choose to have their résumé on two kinds of paper, one for reproduction and one as a statement of taste values. Paper choices are an important part of the designer's toolbox, so naturally the selection for a résumé is a statement in itself.

Be sure that whatever format you use, your layout is clean, logical, and easy to read. Lastly, remember, to write succinctly, with clarity. Make sure your résumé honestly represents your experience, and be careful neither to omit nor exaggerate important responsibilities. Always, always proofread for typos and spelling. Have someone else proof for you as well. Two or three pairs of eyes are best. It can be a killer factor on an otherwise terrific résumé (and can lose you an opportunity).

The sample résumé on the two following pages offers one of many possible solutions. It is clearly meant as a suggested format for a résumé to accompany a portfolio. It will, none-theless, have enough information to "stand alone," or work independently, if submitted by itself. The format is set up to give you instructions within the form of a sample résumé. It is, with a few exceptions, the form we give to applicants in my office when we feel it is needed.

As always, when dealing with résumés or interviews or life in general, what can go wrong will go wrong. I thought it would be amusing, and possibly educational, to tell you of some résumés that would have been better left in a drawer. We collect them under a file called "Résumés I have known but not forgotten."

- Under Skills: "I can do the Rubic's Cube in sixty seconds."
- The Asian designer who, under Foreign Languages, listed "English."
- The recent graduate's résumé took four pages.
- The Special Skill: "Left Handed."
- Under Organizations: The National Association of Floor Covering Women.
- The award for the best closing statement on a covering letter: "I am sixty years of age. My mom is ninety-three, and feeling fine. Dad died of WWI wounds fifty-seven years after having been gassed and shot. My health is excellent and my energy and enthusiasm beyond average."
- Résumés which have a picture covering a least $\frac{1}{4}$ of the page
- The person who had a sex change operation and noted: "born August 23,1949—born again June 12, 1984."
- The proofreader who wrote ". . . support teamwork

SAMPLE RÉSUMÉ
Two pages at most with your last name in the upper right corner of the second page and "Page 2" added and, no pictures, please!

Name
Street Address
City, State, Zip Code
Home phone number
Work (or message) phone number

OBJECTIVE
Only if goals are very specific. Two sentences at most. Consider two résumés, one with and one without objectives. Consider multiple résumés with different objectives.

EXPERIENCE
List your *last* position first (see example below). If you are currently employed, show date as "to present." Job title must be included. Describe the level of your responsibilities (what you really do). Include a client list (who you do it for). The longer you have worked, the less you need to list experiences from more than six to eight years ago. Assume you will get your next position based on your experiences from the last five to eight years. For positions that are before that point, only list the name of firm, your title and perhaps a few clients at most. Be sure to include in your recent work experience description: who you reported to, the quality and level of client contact (middle management, upper management), budgetary or fiscal responsibility, supervision of vendors, support staff freelancers, art direction of illustration and/or photography, and interfacing with copywriters or marketing, any hands-on or direction of computer functions, knowledge of production, and any other applicable points that show responsibility and accountability.

Sample

1990–present	**American Corporation**: Art Director/Designer Responsibilities include design concepts; execution and presentation of design comprehensives; management and supervision of staff of three, freelancers, desktop publishing and computer production staff; selection and art direction of photographers and illustrators; client contact; budget estimates and proposals; and on- press supervision. Projects include all required corporate communications, including company magazines, quarterly reports, press kits, and newsletters.

ENTRY LEVEL APPLICANTS
List all work experience using the same principles as above. Be sure to list first any career-related experiences, such as internships,

summer work, and workshops. Stress experiences that included interpersonal skills (selling, working as a waiter, etc.), or those that required problem-solving, computers, or detail-intensive work.

EDUCATION

College and post-graduate work only. Omit high school. Include special classes or training programs. Be sure to include date of graduation, degree and major.

Sample
> **Pratt Institute:** B.F.A., Graphic Design 1992

SPECIAL SKILLS

Very important for junior and mid-level positions that rely on a high degree of technical expertise. Computer knowledge and software programs must be included.

SPECIAL INTERESTS

Include only if applicable to your job search. Omit hobbies, such as traveling and gourmet cooking. (Everybody is and does.) However, if you are applying for a position on a magazine stressing travel or skiing, your personal interests are important.

PERSONAL

It is preferable to omit personal details unless you want a relocation, at which point marital status and children can become a factor. Birth dates are optional because there are legal restrictions on requesting this information (as well as age, race, and religion) in an interview or application.

AWARDS & PROFESSIONAL RECOGNITION

Always a plus to include if they are recognized industry awards pertinent to your professional life. However, do not include the actual awards in your portfolio.

For example, include awards from higher educational institutions and professional design or advertising organizations, and omit an award for painting in a local show.

REFERENCES

Always state: "Furnished [or available] upon request."

SALARY REQUIREMENTS

Never indicate a salary history or a salary requirement on a résumé. This information can be included in a cover letter, if necessary.

ethic, illicting enthusiastic participation . . ."! This same person went on to say, "Hired two new proofers to replace one unreliable one." (Some proofreading, and what a budget!)

And under the file, "Illiteracies We Have Known" is the person who went to Fairleigh Dickinson University and spelled it "Fairlegh" on our application.

Choosing a Job

Now your job search is becoming effective and you have received an offer from a firm. Once you have gotten over the immediate rush of excitement at a job offer, you need to ask yourself if this position is really the one you want. This is not necessarily an easy question. You will have to consider many conflicting issues. How much do you need to work (it's called paying the rent)? How much do you want to keep your other options open? How much do you like or trust your future employer? But the most important question should be: *Do you want the work produced by that company in your portfolio?* While we'll discuss career building in greater detail in chapter 11, it is important for you to consider some of these issues now, for they cross-reference. The overriding issue should be the knowledge that the quality of work in your portfolio will always determine your next job. It's a simple as that! Therefore, you must always consider that the work you see in the portfolio of a possible employer will be the quality of work entering your portfolio once you work for them. It's not that you won't have some creative freedom, or contribute your talents. It's what the firm's client base is and requires, what the firm's reputation is based on, and how they attract new clients. It is a rare time that you can expect to work on projects which are significantly different than the firm's previous work.

Non-Creative Positions: Account Services, New Business, and Studio Management

These areas offer wonderful and important opportunities for the designer who learns that his or her business, manage-rial, or technical acumen is superior to his or her creative capabilities. It is not uncommon for individuals to experience a reassessment of their skills after a few years in the field. The person who is attracted to account services is the individual who enjoys problem solving and contact with clients more than the actual hands-on process of design. Business development is a highly compensated area for the entrepreneur who can successfully market a sales effort for creative services. Studio managers operate from a knowledge base of production methods and strong organizational skills. All these directions provide key positions in firms with significantly less competition in the hiring process than creative positions. Employers perceive these areas and skills as invaluable components in their organizations and the person who enters these positions with a creative background adds the substantial element of design sensitivity to the position's qualifications. Let's look at them separately.

STUDIO MANAGERS/PRODUCTION MANAGERS

These positions represent a valued component in the design office for it is these individuals who often represent the "glue" that connects the design processes and makes everything happen. These managers must have a strong sense of design, computer technology, printing, and materials. They must have excellent organization skills and generally be detail orientated. Their management of internal personnel, outside vendors, purchasing, budgets, and scheduling makes them ultimately the point-person to insure a project is delivered on time and on budget. Excellent people skills and an equal capacity for verbal and written communication are a must. A firm's profit or loss status can hinge on the skills of the studio or production manager. Salary compensation packages for studio and production managers are usually equivalent to middle management design positions, but this does not mean they cannot rise above that level. Some of these managers eventually become partners in design firms.

ACCOUNT SERVICES/ACCOUNT EXECUTIVES

While these positions are discussed in some detail in chapter 3, account services personnel function in most other areas of the design field as well. *These are the individuals who hone their strategic skills beyond their creative ones.* The designer making a career segue, will find this an important niche in design, for the account team is an integral part of the creative process. Account services offers the opportunity to work with the client in the initial stages of project development, setting the strategy and criteria. It is an intellectually stimulating period in the scope of the project. The account people are often responsible for translating these criteria to the creative staff and all the follow-up liaison work between client and creative. They usually have project responsibility for writing proposals and monitoring budgets. While these positions are not necessarily filled by people with a creative education, they do offer opportunities to designers looking for a career change. Account service managers, account executives, or project managers are middle management or senior management positions and therefore their compensation falls within those ranges.

By the nature of their positions, account people are exposed to the new business development process as practiced by different design consultancies. They are sometimes brought into that process, asked to assist new business efforts or perhaps to expand business by developing additional components to existing projects. Thus they enter the sales arena.

NEW BUSINESS DEVELOPMENT/MARKETING

For some the sales process is totally intimidating. For others it is perceived without fear of rejection and almost as a sport. The ability to market a creative service successfully is the most important component to any design business. Bringing in the business is, of course, critical to any firm's survival. In the past, most new clients came to design offices through the referral process. Firms existed (and still do) by reputation. The past years have seen an expansion of the aggressive marketing of design services. Most firms no longer rely simply on the referral process or on the sole ability of the principals to develop business. Aggressive marketing can include a combination of researchers, telemarketing, account services personnel, and marketing executives devoted solely to the new business effort.

Some of these marketing executives enter design with an MBA degree. They may have had prior experience as a product manager in a corporation or worked in an advertising agency on an account team. However, many of these executives started their careers in design and found they had a knack for the business side. Some moved into this area as designers who became account services executives. Some designers went on to get their MBAs.

Since it is apparent how critical these individuals are to a firm's success, it should be no surprise to know that their compensation is tied to their effectiveness. They are usually paid a salary plus performance-based incentives, most often in the form of commissions. This career track can easily result in an equity position or firm partnership.

Freelancing

What do you do if you don't have too many other options and need to work? Try to consider working on a freelance basis instead of on a staff. The down side is that you won't get health and vacation benefits, but you will be able to continue looking for a better job. What if the employer doesn't want a freelance arrangement? Take the job—but try not to stay too long. Most likely you shouldn't stay more than six months to a year. You'll probably get some good studio experience and be a little more seasoned for the next job search.

Freelancing is an excellent way of sampling a variety of work environments. Although you'll be paid more on an hourly basis than you would on staff, you won't receive benefits, you won't have economic security, and the number of hours you work will be irregular. As it is impossible to live without medical coverage in today's society, be sure you are covered, either by yourself or through a family member. Many people like to freelance because of the sheer diversity of experience in the work environment, the flexible hours, and the tax benefits they receive from the IRS as an "independent." This is a good time to get some expert advice from an accountant who can instruct you on the proper forms of

Tax Benefits

record-keeping. When you are freelancing, you are self-employed and therefore entitled to the business expenses attached with being self-employed. It can be an excellent way of life for the more independent soul. It also means going without the security of a full-time position and not feeling a part of a team. Freelancing on a temporary basis serves well for the person who is holding out for the "perfect" job, or for the person who wants a break from moving from one permanent position to another. It also represents an excellent solution to bad economic periods. When jobs are scarce, there is always an increase of freelance opportunities. Freelancing can serve an additional purpose when it allows both company and employee to get used to each other. Some possibilities are a trial period before a full-time offer is extended, or the proverbial "foot in the door" opportunity at a highly desirable firm. From the employer's viewpoint it's often used as a method of "try before you buy."

The Foot in the Door

Individuals with their own electronic set-ups have established an important niche market by offering a new range of choices to employers with flexible staffing needs. This is the bedrock of the "virtual office" in which talent can be accessed on an as-needed basis. A cottage industry has developed for these individuals, many of whom are parents who can take full advantage of working at home. The flexibility of these arrangements services everyone's requirements; work is often sent by modem; and the result is a win-win situation.

A negative aspect to freelancing, however, is the consideration that the process rarely contributes anything substantial to a person's portfolio. Most often you will be asked to work on the implementation of assignments, instead of seeing them from beginning to end. There is hardly an opportunity to put work into your portfolio that shows any real personal contribution or impact. If you freelance for too long (more than a year or eighteen months) the results could be damaging to your portfolio should you choose to return to a permanent position. After a time your work would become dated and you could have difficulty showing what you did for that period of time. There are, of course, people who are permanent freelancers. In this instance we need to make distinctions between freelancing and being self-employed. The subtle nuance is the assumption that after a prolonged period the individual is really self-employed (although there may be no other employees working for the individual) and truly

Will Your Portfolio Benefit?

committed to independent status. If, for economic or other reasons, work dries up and the designer wants a staff position, we have great difficulty placing people. While the foremost reason maybe the structure of their portfolio, there is always a latent suspicion in the employer's mind that the candidate will return to a freelance or independent status as soon as it's viable. This is a realistic acknowledgment of the different goals of independent designers who are very content with the lifestyle and income afforded through their freelance business. Certainly it is an option to consider as one of the many paths available. ■

Are You Self-Employed?

10

Your Portfolio

Your portfolio is your most important expression of everything you are and want to be. It is a unique display of your talent and an exhibit of your experience. While it is a visual expression, it demonstrates a psychological shorthand that must tell your special story. And since life experiences or personal histories are never alike, it follows that no two portfolios are alike. How individual the portfolios are is a constant fascination to all those who are in a position to review many "books" (in the jargon of our business). They are analogous to human faces, which have some similar characteristics, but are never actually the same. The structure of portfolios must always be flexible, always subject to the needs of the individual, but should express in the best possible way what you have done, what you can do, and what you want to do. *It is therefore the visual embodiment of your past, present, and future.*

Accepting this portentous pronouncement, is it any wonder that the content and presentation of a portfolio is, without question, the single most anxiety-producing element and the most critical part in the entire job search process? While I have gone to great lengths to show how important every other element of your persona is, and that your ability to be successful is not totally dependent upon your visual talent, it is nonetheless your portfolio that makes it all possible. It will get you in the door, after which your other skills must take charge. Remember, in the vast majority of application processes, your work will precede your persona as an introduction. Often you will drop off your portfolio or send transparencies of your work (see chapter 9, Getting Started). Without the talent and its proper presentation the rest is simply not possible. And to compound the pressure placed on this "simple" book, the number of people who lose opportunities not due to their talent but because of the condition of their portfolio is simply astonishing. It is not only astonishing but sometimes cruel, for without a knowledgeable person pointing the way, many get lost. We have seen many people hired because we insisted on an interview after the portfolio had been rejected. We accomplish this difficult task only because of the level of confidence we command as recruiters. Lack of information or misinformation can counteract years of valuable study and training. Obviously, this chapter will not only point the way, but give you some important insights into how people evaluate the look of portfolios when they need to hire.

Format

Many people like to be rather dogmatic about the construction of a portfolio. Examples would include dictums as to how one should only use boards or perhaps certain kinds of folios. Others advise that your portfolio should stand out from the crowded masses of black books and make a statement! They advise that you should construct a unique, personalized statement.

While we have reviewed many unique, wonderful books, our experience has shown that attempts at these unusual constructions have proven to be disastrous in most cases. A trip to any fully stocked art supply store will quickly confirm the selection available is so large, that the number of choices and the selection process is difficult enough. The critical decisions regarding your portfolio format should relate to content and ability to provide you with a flexible system. You need to analyze the essence of your work. Is it primarily two- or three-dimensional, or is it interactive? Is the two-dimensional work flat or does it include pamphlets and brochures? Would the three-dimensional work be best served through photography? Interactive work can be viewed on line, by disk, Syquest, Zip-drivers, or CD-ROM. Which not only works best but, importantly, will the viewer have the proper technology to access? It's important to call ahead and check. If you are using a Zip drive, you may want to bring it along. Remember if you have your résumé on any of these, be sure to include a paper copy. Maybe there will be times that you need a combination of formats to adequately show phases of a project. You need to approach your portfolio with a knowledge of what is logical for the specific problem and not feel locked into a format. There are no rules as to right or wrong. The only rule is that what "works" makes for success. And you must give clear consideration to size.

Size

Somehow the size factor is often the last to be considered. However, size also affects weight. Therefore you should think about how you will feel carrying your book, looking for work for perhaps days, weeks, or months. How will it hold up on buses, trains, subways, and planes? How will it fare in bad weather? Is it waterproof? Since the use of a messenger service may sometimes be necessary, would you want the service to refuse to carry it because it's too heavy? Would you want to see your portfolio have to be checked in at an airport? Will it fit into an overhead compartment on a plane? Would you ever have to ship your portfolio? In that case, size will affect cost.

Will you want two portfolios? Often it helps to have either a duplicate or books that serve different purposes. Duplicate portfolios can have a variety of purposes, not the least being the safety factor of not ever losing everything that is the key to your future. You should protect yourself by documenting your work through photography. We have experienced occasions in which books were lost, and the results are heartbreaking. One recent graduate lost her portfolio in a subway. She simply forgot to take it with her when she got off the train. Another person left his portfolio in the taxi that dropped him off in front of our office. He was, however, able to get it back through the Taxi and Limousine Commission.

And it can happen to experienced travelers too. A call was placed to me from a baggage handler in Chicago's O'Hare Airport saying that he had a small case with slides, an address book in German, and my business card as the only identification (he could read). I was able to identify it as belonging to an individual on the way to a major conference presentation! This, of course, also makes a case for properly identifying your belongings. Portfolios have been lost through moving, accidents, and fire. Don't let it ever happen to you. I must add that only once in over ten years did we ever have a client lose a book. It happened at a large advertising agency. Most firms, ours included, have tightly controlled systems for logging books in and out. While you must protect yourself from accidents, do not let the fear of losing your portfolio prevent you from dropping your work off to be seen. Occasionally we encounter someone who refuses to leave their book, insisting on an interview. The net result of that attitude is to be cut off from opportunities.

For some reason students seem to have the largest portfolios. In contrast there seems to be a equation that *the more experienced the designer, the smaller the book*. One graphic designer has his portfolio on a series of small, Formica-like chips held together by a key chain. Another person reduced his presentation to a four-by-five box of transparencies, presented like a deck of cards. While these examples demonstrate an individualization of presentation and a move away from the "black book" standard, I mention them because their realized objective was to condense as well as personalize. The message is, size bears no relation to content. Size also seems to bear no relation to the person carrying it. We often are amazed to see the smallest individuals bringing in books that we can't lift!

Choosing a Format

So, what works? Boards are heavy. Acetate scratches. Transparencies can be expensive. You need to be wary of disks that are not technically compatible or that the person viewing them is technically up to speed. And what about a group of samples that greatly vary in size? While there are no absolute answers the following are some suggestions based on current modes. When deciding on size consider the average of most of your pieces and work within that framework. Oversized pieces such as posters should be reduced by utilizing four-by-five transparencies.

When having your work photographed, get it done as professionally as possible. If you are in school, seek out in-school photo services or photography majors. Most working designers know someone who can do them a favor. Obviously the quality of the photography means everything. It is awkward to have to apologize for poorly photographed work during an interview. It also sends a negative message.

Transparencies work nicely when mounted in black board frames and have become, if costs permit, the preferred method of presentation. Three-dimensional work, packaging, exhibition, and industrial design should all be photographed. You can combine 35mm slides and four-by-five transparencies—sometimes even on the same mounting board, if it makes sense. And you should combine photographed work with the actual pieces or sketches when appropriate. At least a sampling of actual printed material should always be included, for people want to touch, smell, and feel the finished product. Slides most often lose much of the impact of the typography as well as any sense of the paper and quality of printing. However, slides do have the advantage of hiding the rough edges on hand work. Anything drawn or cut and pasted always looks better when photographed and reduced. Remembering to periodically document your work—through slides, finished, and rough art—as a safety measure against loss is advice worth repeating.

Sketches

It is impossible to overstate the importance of including sketches in your portfolio, even in this age of digitized production. The critical significance of sketches is often underrated by the designer who doesn't understand or appreciate the integral value of sketch books, roughs, and comps. Therefore they should definitely be included in the back of your book and must be saved from the waste paper basket at work. Many people cringe when asked to include what are often messy sketches. Don't worry. (I had one creative director say "I don't care if they're torn and full of coffee stains. I have to see how he works and thinks!") They should be placed in a neat folder and labeled appropriately. They are a key ingredient in your presentation, for they indicate the process of your thoughts, your act of problem-solving, the variety of scope of your thinking, and often exhibit a preferable realization of a solution to the finished product shown in your book (if they have been killed by a client or proven too impractical). Your sketches show the breadth of your imagination. They are the key to the essence of your fundamental creative personality. While I may risk redundancy, I feel I cannot stress sufficiently the importance of not being computer dependent and the importance of demonstrating your drawing, typographic, and conceptual abilities through these sketches. No person that I truly respect would view a book and not expect to see these drawings.

Finished Art

Flat print work, editorial, identity programs, packaging design, and labels are most often displayed in a spiral or bound acetate book in which the pages can be moved or replaced. The quality of acetate has improved and scratching is not as much of a problem as in the past, but it still exists. No one has yet developed ring binders which close so tightly that they will not catch the pages as you turn them. Just remember, no matter what format you choose, your presentation should be immaculate. If necessary, you must replace the acetate as needed. Never show anything that's dirty or dog-eared. When including a sample that has multiple pages, such as a brochure or annual report, freestanding acetate sleeves both protect your work and make the entire project accessible to the viewer. If you want to include a publication in which you were responsible for only certain pages, tabbing or clipping the work becomes an acceptable method. Since you will most likely be asked to drop off your portfolio, you may want to include a written description, index of the portfolio's contents, or labels on certain items. Remember, though, the résumé accompanying your work will indicate your level of responsibility. Please also remember to label everything that could possibly be separated. Your name must be on anything that could be taken out or fall out.

Presentation

Everything you include in your book says something to the viewer about your personality, talent, and attitudes toward work. How you treat your work tells the viewer not only how you respect your own work, but how you will respect your future employer's projects. Needless to say, your presentation must be of the highest caliber. It sounds obvious and simple, but you can't imagine how many portfolios we see that do not fulfill these requirements. Some people literally throw work into a portfolio and just zip it up. Whatever format you choose for presentation, it has to be clean, logical, and flexible in order to reflect your interests. As to its flexibility and order of presentation, you must consider everything discussed in this passage along with the suggestions made in chapter 9, for the two are completely interrelated. One relates to the inner self, the other to the outward manifestation of that self. In order to tailor your presentation to the firms you approach, you need the physical capability to communicate the inner reality.

I always suggest that the first project exposed to the viewer when they open your portfolio is your best. It is your initial introduction. You really do have a few important seconds to create a first impression. Your "hello," appearance, and handshake set the tone for all that follows. So too does the first piece in your portfolio. The tone should be one of excitement and anticipation for all that is to follow. It sets the stage. It dictates the psychological atmosphere that will predispose the viewer's thinking to your other work. This is the very important psychological "shorthand" mentioned in the first paragraph of this chapter. You must create an anticipation that your book is going to be a wonderful experience for the viewer. After that, you must follow with the most appropriate work for the particular situation and end with a piece almost as good as the piece with which you started.

Why the Sequence Is Critical

Everyone always wants to know how many pieces to include in a portfolio. As usual there are no magic formulas, but a portfolio shouldn't have fewer than ten to twelve samples of projects and probably no more than fifteen to eighteen. If you have twenty, you probably have gone too far. This is clearly a case of quality and not quantity. *The old adage that your portfolio is as strong as the weakest piece in it is absolutely true!* It is amazing how often a person is

How Many Samples?

**Consistency
and Style**

refused an interview because one or two pieces were included that should have been left in the drawer. Try to include as many projects as possible that show implementation of an idea or a campaign. The implementation of a project should be considered as part of the whole project and therefore not count as additional samples in your book. Ideas that show many components and applications are better that a single solution with a single purpose. Consistency is a tremendous characteristic of a well-composed book. *Inconsistency is perceived as lack of taste or lack of focus.* Both characteristics are frowned upon and have a negative effect. The concept of consistency in showing a body of creative work is a subjective and abstract process. Any critique of work is, by its nature, totally subjective. However, developing consistency in the level or quality of the work is a separate issue from consistency in the type of projects shown.

We are all familiar with the question of style. Most well-known fine artists or graphic design icons of this century have a style that is easily recognized. We can spot a Rauchenberg or Warhol in a minute. We all know Paul Rand's work. But could we recognize all the stylistic changes in Milton Glaser's work over the years? It is a question of consistency of approach versus a personal style.

The strongest portfolios show a consistency of approach toward design. But we need to consider what to show a prospective employer. The book also needs to address specific business directions. Therefore the difficult balance must include a consistency of projects specific to a business direction. To this end, how does your book address the prospective firm's business focus? What do they do and how do they do it? Therefore what do you show? I have always believed in the philosophy that people see what they want to see. So I recommend establishing a (marketplace) consistency of business direction in the portfolio. It is the reality of the marketplace that creates these demands. We discussed why one needs a flexible format. This is the optimum moment to utilize that flexibility. Some of our tricks of the trade are to often rearrange work, delete or add if the missing links are available to produce a whole response which:

- reflects your individual goals
- reflects your level of talent and experience
- functions logically to the needs of the marketplace.

When we hear of a job opening, we will ask a person whether he or she is interested in submitting work. We will describe the position in detail. If the designer wants to be considered as a candidate, we may, if we think it's necessary, ask them to show X, Y, and Z; delete S and T; and ask if they perhaps have some samples of R that would be appropriate in relation to the job. However, as a general modus operandi, we will not show any work if we feel it's not up to the client's standards.

Since a "tight" and objective sampling of your own work is extremely difficult to achieve, try to get private criticism from as many people as possible by showing your book to those whom you respect. While it is unlikely that they will all agree, you should get a general consensus to consider. Ultimately, it must be your decision as to what to include. However, beware of emotionally attaching yourself to projects that were very difficult or involved a great deal of work. They are hard to let go of and exclude, but they may not be the best representation of your work. It's a similar syndrome to in the decisionmaking process of choosing a field of endeavor. (See chapter 9, Who Are You?) At the same time, you should always have the confidence to stick to those beliefs in which you have a strong conviction.

Changing Work Goals

Often a person wants to diversify his/her experiences and to change his/her goals or field of specialty. This is a wonderful way of staying fresh. An example would be a person who has spent several years working on magazines and decides he or she "wants out" of editorial design. The challenge presented by this type of shift is a portfolio that has become very specialized. As stated, most often people see what they want to see. This means that if they are seeking a packaging designer, they want to see packaging. For a designer to merely express an "interest" in working in that field is simply not enough to demonstrate the ability, nor will a passing knowledge or a few packaging projects do the trick. The only way I have seen a career segue possible is when:

- The designer makes a strong attempt to find freelance work in the area of choice and then include it in the book.

- The designer reworks existing projects into another format or includes "spec" work demonstrating his or her ability in the area of choice.
- There exists some logical connection within the essential character of the work. Examples would include utilizing the art direction of fashion photography toward another art direction job or perhaps an editorial designer moving into annual reports.
- Personal persuasion: A person is somehow able to convince another to give the designer a chance.

In any case, the common denominator is to put "other" work into your book that will clearly demonstrate your flexibility as a designer. It is difficult and takes enormous effort to develop "new" work or samples, especially when you have a full-time job. However, it is a way to make change possible for you.

Although I often make these recommendations, few people have the energy follow them. Some years ago, however, I suggested this approach to an editorial designer who wanted to be considered for a position at a sales promotional agency. I knew they'd never seriously consider someone from, in this case, a computer magazine. The designer took my advice and reworked some of his editorial spreads by cutting and pasting them into promotion pieces. He did a splendid job and was hired.

Shared Projects and Work Ethics

The content guidelines outlined here obviously apply to samples from either work experience or from school projects. In any discussion of portfolio content, the question of shared projects or projects that have had a strong collaborative input must be addressed. As a young designer you may find yourself working on a project in which the concept or art direction has been set. You may be asked to do the type specifications, crop photos, work within an established grid or pagination, and so forth. Yet that contribution is important and the work deserves to be included. Ethically, your résumé should indicate the level of your responsibility and in an interview you should indicate what your role was on a given project.

Our clients sometimes complain about "duplicate" portfolios. Perhaps they are seeing more than one person from the
same firm. This becomes a sticky wicket when the individuals
work on the same level and there is no clear reporting structure. An example would be two or three art directors leaving
a firm who worked for the same client. If the same projects
appear in each portfolio, it's natural to raise questions of
conflict. As long as you clearly represent your role in a
project there shouldn't be any inquiries requiring you to
validate your contribution. When you don't clearly represent
your role, the fallout can be quite destructive. Any misrepre-
sentation weakens everyone's position. The worst condemna-
tion is the phrase "I don't think the work is his." The word
"think" casts a long shadow. Once you are questioned, it is
hard to get into the clear light again.

Duplicate
Samples

This subject is appropriate, on a more complicated level,
to senior-level staff leaving a firm to start their own business.
Their ability to present their past work is key to establishing
their credentials to new clients. Any designer should have the
freedom to demonstrate experience and creativity, and this is
generally accepted by the industry, as long as the work
shown is accurately described. The bottom line is to be
completely honest and fully describe the conditions under
which any work was done, crediting the appropriate firms or
individuals. If there is a dispute, legal action will often
follow. (See chapter 11, Hiring Practices.)

The Ethics of
Assigning Credit

Today, we perceive a renewed emphasis on business ethics
as having significance and value. This represents another
aspect of the 1990s backlash to the "any method that is
profitable is acceptable" attitudes of the 1980s. The designer,
whose career is built on individual creativity, must always
recognize the need to protect that individuality in a business
world that often structures work through team efforts. The
designer needs to establish a delicate balance between being
a "team player" and a creative "individualist." At the end of
the day, your talent and personal reputation are all you have.

In the 1990s these are both old-fashioned and new-
fashioned values. Fortunately for some, they never changed.
To cut corners for expediency's sake is ultimately to cut off
opportunities. It's an old platitude, but true, that the world is
very round. I have seen business opportunities lost because of
word on the "street" about "indiscretions" made many years
before. The individuals losing the opportunities are never

told why and probably would never associate it with a long gone, past history. The dangers of this word of mouth or innuendo is clear. Perhaps it's true, or perhaps not—but it exists.

Avoiding Negative Reputations

There is another dimension to the negative fallout of questionable business ethics. Many designers will not take a job with a firm whose reputation is in doubt. The industry "grapevine" is very powerful. Often, the telling points are how much turnover a firm may be experiencing. We have witnessed expressions of this syndrome when designers leave jobs because of disapproval of the owners' methods of doing business. Since our subject is creatively driven businesses, those firms are, in the last analysis, significantly hurt by a cutoff of their prime resource, creative talent.

In short, mistakes made in your twenties or thirties can follow you into your forties and fifties. Value yourself, value your reputation, and others will hold the same opinion. It's not being a Pollyanna, it's good business. Ultimately, we may discuss ethics and to what degree one is "comfortable" within a given situation; but even for the most pragmatic of business people, the bottom line is the ability to maintain the "critical mass" of the business. In short, no one wants to diminish their business because of incorrect ethical decisions.

Production Work in a Creative Book

Sometimes the designer, especially in a first job, will be asked to do mundane, non-creative work. Perhaps you may have taken a job doing production on work you don't like, but the job at that time was necessary. In other words, you may have worked on projects you won't want to include as part of your portfolio, but, nonetheless, you have spent a significant time at that job. It shows on your résumé and you don't want it to represent your level of creativity. The solution to this quandary is to put the work into your portfolio, but into a rear pocket or a separate folder. It should be marked "production" and may be next to another, similar folder marked "sketches." It still represents a quality of experience that should positively add to the body of your work. By separating it out, it will not conflict with your creative persona.

Still Can't Make the Final Content Decisions?

When all else fails in trying to decide which samples to delete, I suggest the following: Take six or seven pieces, lay them out for comparison, and delete the weakest one. Now do the same with five or six other pieces. Shuffle the remaining samples together and repeat the process. In this manner you will constantly cut down the number of samples as you increase the quality.

Why Your Portfolio Will Never Be Finished

I'm sure you can understand the rationale behind this statement. You may not realize that some designers do consider their portfolios finished. It is a mistake to do so. Just as there are designers who can never quite deliver a completed book because they are so enthusiastic about their "latest" project just coming off press that must be included, there are those who are perfectly content to present the same book to everyone for all purposes and for a long time. Clearly it is this person who is "stuck" in time, never growing or being able to demonstrate something new.

Your portfolio should always to be considered as a work in progress, representing the last five years or so of your work experiences. You should always be thinking about updating it and wrestling with the process of addition and deletion. As you grow professionally, your attitudes, point of view, and creative style will grow as well. New jobs, new interests, and new perspectives will all flavor the content of your portfolio. Your portfolio is a current and demanding diary of your work and personality. It always requires your care and attention. And while you must keep it current, never discard the past. Keep it filed. It will become a valuable personal history. I hope you'll enjoy these souvenirs as much as you'll enjoy your future. ■

11

Hiring Practices

Looking for work with a realistic expectation means recognizing the full scope of the dynamics at play. It means having a "big picture" viewpoint and thinking beyond your own objectives. Otherwise you will get lost in the trap of a consuming, subjective experience in which your agenda seems to be the only issue. Most individuals are so wrapped up with their own priorities, they do not focus on what may be the primary need of the employer (the very person with whom they desire to develop a relationship). For that matter, many employers can only focus on their immediate dilemma of finding someone to fill a specific spot and solve their pressing problems. Rarely do they remember how they felt when they were looking for a job.

Establishing Business Relationships

The key ingredient for a successful relationship is the synergy that develops between employer and employee. The only way that can be accomplished is for the employer and prospective employee to recognize and understand each other's point of view. For the candidate looking for work, understanding the employer's needs is the first step toward creating that relationship. Often it will also spell success in the job search. The employer's recognition of the candidate's goals completes this equation.

It is my belief that the quality of these employee/employer relationships defines both of their futures. Their relationship also defines the quality of the product they produce. The quality of the end product will determine the success of the firm and the future career paths of the individuals involved. Employer and employee should recognize the essential fact that, in a creatively driven business, *people are the inventory and they walk out the door every night.* Therefore the level of

Guideposts to Success ... talent and commitment possessed by the employee or demanded by the employer establishes the internal synergy of the relationship and the profound power one has over the other. This synergy controls the essential give and take in a creative business relationship. The possible issues of personality, office politics, ambition, work environment, sex, culture, title, money, work ownership, the quality of the work and clients, and many other more subtle elements create the dynamics of successful or unsuccessful relationships. These components are key guideposts in making decisions when questions of hiring, firing, leaving, or taking a position need to be acted on. Most people erroneously discount the role of personality and emotionalism in the decisionmaking process, and both employer and employee may assume that position and money are the motivating ingredients. The extent and variety of these issues should always be factored into your thinking and you will approach situations with a far more pragmatic and sophisticated outlook.

If there is an inability for both sides to maintain this strategic business relationship, their lack of synchronization

... and Failure can contribute to the decline of the company. There are dramatic examples of how firms have been crippled by the loss of key talent who left for greener pastures. The issues at work are more often creative freedom and recognition than title and money. A significant example dates from 1987 and while that is, for some, ancient history, it still is a dramatic example. Lord Geller Frederico Einstein, a New York agency of major reputation, which was part of J. Walter Thompson and owned by the WPP Group, was shattered by the defection of much of its creative staff. Both partners and employees left, claiming lack of creative freedom, and formed Lord

Einstein O'Neill & Partners with Young & Rubicam as the parent company. The move placed the valuable IBM contract in jeopardy. Today, after a landmark lawsuit in favor of the parent WPP Group, Lord Einstein O'Neill & Partners does not exist, the highly valued accounts have flown to other agencies, and many lives and careers have been unalterably changed and some destroyed.

In the Beginning: The Hiring

The creative relationship between employer and employee begins in the hiring process. This can be fragile, dependent on a special synergy and ending when one of the two breaks away for another goal. Both parties participate in an important pas de deux: joining together in a creative effort in which the quality of the choreography determines the success of the business as well as their careers.

The beginning is the formation of hiring policies and procedures that combine these talents into successful business partnerships (and sometimes the development of important mentor relationships). The dynamics of this subject are often discussed only behind closed doors and rarely in print. Nonetheless, these difficult questions are critical to anyone developing a career:

- How do the decisions get made on both sides of the fence?
- What are the priorities and criteria that determine hiring policies and the acceptance of the employee?
- What are the underlying agendas?
- Just what is the "chemistry" of a successful interview?

Critical honesty is as rare a response as it is a painful process. Furthermore, it can be a dangerous course, as it can make the individual vulnerable to all sorts of retaliatory actions. Due to the subjectivity of many decisions and the general unwillingness of employers to say anything negative about an individual, the focus is shifted elsewhere during interviews or in conversation with recruiters. The true concerns don't surface and the person only experiences rejection without constructive feedback. Although this dynamic can be very subtle, in the role of the "headhunter" I see many examples every day pointing out how crucial (and sometimes damaging) these factors can be to both parties. Therefore I'd like to point out the following:

- Anyone interviewing should always consider and respect the other's point of view and agenda.
- Anyone who has ever been in a position to hire staff knows the choices that are made affect the reputation and creative work of the entire group.
- Anyone looking for work should recognize how important that next job is toward their career development and future employment.

Tables can turn rapidly in business. Everyone should recognize and remember what it means to be in the other's place. Too often we find that our most cooperative applicant becomes the most unnecessarily demanding client or the difficult, inaccessible client turns suddenly into the vulnerable job seeker. Therefore, we should remember what it is to walk in another's shoes, and so:

- Anyone who makes hiring decisions should recognize that the decisionmaking seat can quickly be turned into the applicant's chair.

  Hiring is about choices, priorities, and decisions— and what drives people to make them. It's also about how important these decisions are.
- How the structuring and hiring policies of an office can be the key to its growth.
- How the relationships can be maintained and nurtured for the sharing of success.
- How careers can be nurtured.
- How not to blow an important interview.
- What people in positions of power really want from an employee.
- How reputations can be made or broken.
- How the players commence their dance and, sometimes, why it ends.

The Employer's Viewpoint

Candidates under consideration for a position always ask us what the "feedback" was and often sincerely desire constructive criticism. Most employers do not want to take the time and make the effort to comment constructively. As discussed, if the criticism is negative it's especially distasteful to criticize. However, the standard response we receive is: "it's just not right," or, perhaps, "it's not a fit." Understandably, designers find it hard to face these ambiguous responses. However, the word "fit" does tell a significant story. Fit means everything. It relates to everything previously mentioned, from "tailoring" a portfolio to meeting client needs and expectations. It also tells more about certain expectations that sometimes are not accurately expressed in job descriptions. The firm is seeking appropriateness.

Let's step back and consider what happens when a company determines they need to hire. The first driving force will be the work load. During the very difficult recession that began in 1989, virtually every company reassessed their employment needs. The majority went through various modes of downsizing and restructuring, contributing to the development of a lexicon of corporate-speak terms that have become a hallmark of corporate insensitivity to the resulting human dilemma of middle management. The net effect for most corporations today is a structure in which the work force has transcended the "lean and mean" phase and which, in many ways, represents a healthier work environment, with accountability a key ingredient to a successful and profitable climate. No company can afford or tolerate individuals who do not have clear responsibility and a rational role. Gone are scores of employees whose roles represented built-in redundancies. The body of the remaining work force is made up of people who are flexible team players, ready to assume a variety of functions. In many cases job descriptions were written to combine jobs or articulate the need for people who were more knowledgeable of the "big picture" and were generally more sophisticated.

The Lean Workplace

The kind of person who will enter this lean workplace is therefore another key component in the newly augmented hiring criteria. The 1990s has produced a market for the educated talent who is not "just creative." There has been a general acceleration in the past few years for individuals who understand the broader scope of the job, department, or firm. Creative talent must understand the business of the business and recognize that design is only a tool for information that communicates a marketing strategy or image.

The question of who gets hired and why is often answered by the ability of creative people to verbally, as well as visually,

Who Gets Hired

articulate these principles. In a very competitive marketplace how and why hiring decisions are made is the critical point of concern. What are employers looking for? What will make them choose one person over another? While we began to explore some of the answers in the preceding paragraph, that is not the whole story. The overriding common thread in job descriptions focuses on personality and the ability to be a team player. Time and again we are requested to find individuals who can not only contribute on the highest level of creativity, but who can contribute to the group as a whole. It's a constant quest for the "perfect person" who can assume a leadership role (if senior) or have the potential for more responsibility than the position calls for, but can also function as a member of the team. Promotabilty is a factor. It is far more desirable to find the individual who can go the long course, staying and growing with the firm. Many companies prefer to hire at lower levels, train and "grow" their own.

And nobody wants high-strung creative egos. I cannot stress how often these same words are repeated by vastly different firms. Strong egos and temperaments are not welcome. No firm wants a disruptive personality within its work group. It is necessary to make clear, however, we are not diminishing the person who has a strong vision or opinions. The key is how opinions are communicated to others.

It may be a surprise to some that minority considerations are never an issue. All employers are legally bound by state and federal laws. Graphic design is truly color blind as the portfolio usually precedes the individual. The demographics of the business probably would show (there hasn't been a survey in many years) an increase of Asians and women and a very small percentage of African Americans.

Work Ethic Another important criteria is the work ethic. Everyone who is successful (without exception) is highly dedicated to the quality of the product and willing to put in whatever effort is required to make the product as perfect as possible, on time and within budget. This is not an easy objective, but a necessary one. In this aspect the fundamental criteria are motivation and quality. The "good" people are manic about quality and are obsessively unrelenting. This all translates into a passion for one's work. While passion can be stimulated by challenge, it cannot be learned and all too few have it. It's a characteristic not readily found but instantly recognized and appreciated.

These value-added characteristics and requirements are all in addition to the importance of individual creativity and various technical skills necessary for employment. They are the fundamental deal makers or deal breakers in hiring decisions. These attitudes cannot be communicated through the portfolio. Your portfolio, remember, is just your introduction to a firm. It is the first cut on screening out individuals. It moves you up to the short list. It is during the interview that your attitudes and personality traits must become evident. If the appropriate questions are not being asked, you must aggressively address these issues. You must be able to communicate your awareness of business issues, work priorities, and your personal dedication into any conversations about your work or portfolio.

Summary

To summarize what employers want, the following is a classical listing of skills and personality requirements made by employers, large and small, when giving my firm a hiring request. It is a time when they can, in candor and off the record, vent their frustrations. I use the word "frustrations," because when looking for work you rarely consider that the employer is often at his or her wit's end trying to find someone with the necessary skills! In any case, the following is a list of characteristic requests made by employers in a majority of current job descriptions for people at different levels of expertise:

- Talent: always first, but never enough by itself.
- Business savvy: innate understanding of the firm's objectives.
- Smart: not just I.Q. but street smarts too.
- Commitment: to quality and the need for perfection.
- Motivation: toward the firm and getting the job done.
- Verbal skills: able to articulate the design process to client and staff alike and participate in client presentations.
- Appearance: looking professional, representing the company. (We have observed many instances in which a candidate got the job because their appearance contributed to the nature of the job and the image of the firm. I need to make the distinction that these are legitimate factors and not those based on sexism.)
- Organizational skills: able to establish priorities, supervise others, control budgets.
- Technology: hands-on or if in a supervisory role, a

significant understanding of current technology for printing, paper, alternative forms of digital media, and production, as well as a commitment to remain current.

- Writing skills: the ability to contribute or originate written proposals.
- Flexibility: no job description can say it all. The ability to roll with the punches, wear whichever hat is necessary, pitch in, do the job, fill the void.
- Attitude: and do it all cheerfully, always working as a team player.
- References: a general reputation for accountability on the job.

The Candidate's Viewpoint

Impossible requests? Not really. The above list of characteristics defines virtually every successful person I know. While you will not be expected to do it all on your first job, you will at least recognize the road ahead and aspire to those goals. However, you can perhaps understand how difficult it is to find "ideal" employees. As one of my clients stated with a sigh: "Good people are not difficult to find—they're impossible to find!"

Well, what about the other side of this equation? What do designers want when they are looking for work? Why do they want to leave a job? What's going wrong? Why are they frustrated, too? The following is a listing of motivating factors I've observed though the years:

- Professional growth: People will either not take a job or will leave if professional growth is blocked by others in the company.
- Quality of clients: Designers recognize that the level or nature of the work will affect their future work. They want to work for an organization that will defend good creative work and fight for the right decisions.
- Need for diversity: Most designers desire a variety in their work experience. Sometimes they may leave a specialized job after a while to find diversity or move toward another goal.
- Recognition: A common frustration is the failure of employers to recognize effort. This recognition may be

demonstrated in traditional ways with title and money, but often the lack stems from a very personal need for the "pat on the back."

- Money: What a job is worth is the crux of this issue. The financial realities of the marketplace and questions of employee value are the heart of the problem. Salaries differ substantially due to the size of the firm, the nature of the work, the geographical location, and the cost of living. Some firms pay what they think they can get away with, and some what they think they have to. Some corporate salaries are tightly scheduled by restrictive compensation scales often determined and evaluated by outside compensation consultants. These salaries are scheduled within a range allocated to the job description and do not allow for much flexibility or negotiation. Employees sometimes have erroneous ideas of their worth or perhaps no idea at all if they have been working at one place for a long time. However, this is of key importance when accepting a position or leaving one. See chapter 12, The Money Question.

- Lifestyle: There seems to be a new outlook on the meaning and form a quality lifestyle can take today, in contrast to five to ten years ago. Many individuals are focusing on family and the amount of leisure time available. Therefore the relevant issues of length of commute, amount of overtime, holidays, vacation time, and relocation to other geographical environments arise. The need to put in unusual overtime is often a reason for leaving a job or not taking it.

- Children and Parental care: Recent years have witnessed a significant increase in concerns for aging parents or the care for children (especially in the rising number of single parent families). These concerns become factors in employment decisions especially relating to relocation, overtime, and full- or part-time employment issues. The Family Leave Act provides job security without pay should a family emergency arise.

- Opportunity: The best reason to take a job is opportunity and the best reason to leave a job is lack of opportunity. For the ambitious, nothing replaces the ability to realize one's goals. We have seen many individuals make a lateral move (accepting the same salary) as well as step back (take less) in title and salary because the new job was perceived as an opportunity to move forward.

- Position: Often the way to move up is by moving out. It is very common to leave a job because of a logical need to change responsibilities, title, and/or salary. The individual can feel blocked in his or her present job because of the structure of the firm (for example, it can be too small or too large to offer the next step up). Or perhaps there is someone in that coveted job who is not going to leave, or the employer does not recognize the need for promotion. The complaint is often "There's just no place to go!"

The New Feminine Majority

- Women's Issues: The demographics of design are heavily weighted towards women. For reasons not completely clear, graphic design is overwhelmingly female for those under forty years old. Employers will need to accommodate women who want a family and a career. While there is a slow movement toward flexible hours (flex time) and maternity leave (for men too), at the time of this writing it is strictly token (see chapter 9, Benefits). Talented women will not want to accept positions not offering maternity leave. Several have indicated the desire for four-day work weeks. This picture is a changing one that I feel will play a stronger role in hiring issues as this work force matures.

There are other hiring factors to consider in any discussion of women in graphic design.

- Pay Scales: Women are not always paid as much as men. Sometimes the cause falls at the feet of women. They simply do not ask for as much money. This may be caused by a lack of security or lack of aggressive negotiation skills. I'm not sure. However, this condition will certainly change, since time is on the side of a maturing and growing female work force. They will be assuming the senior positions of the future.
- Travel: As the world economy grows, many positions focus on extended travel. This can be difficult for those with young families.
- Personal: Many employers are in open admiration of and court the woman in the marketplace. If you refer back to our employers' wish list, you'll note the em-

phasis on flexibility and verbal skills. Women seem to excel in these areas. Perhaps it's because they are raised to assume so many roles and wear all those hats? In any case, savvy employers recognize these important traits.

- Harassment: Simply put, harassment exists and can take many forms. When possible, and when it's recognized, most people will change jobs rather than try to make a change in the workplace. Harassment can be physical (unusual work loads or extra-long hours), sexual, racial, or psychological (applying unnecessary pressure, destroying self-confidence). The protagonist is usually playing power politics or is simply a tyrant or bully. Some employers have been classified as "screamers" or "throwers" by people we have interviewed. A warning light would be an unusually high rate of turnover for employees in the firm. When too many employees come and go, some firms get reputations for being "revolving doors," and, while it can be for other reasons, subtle or overt harassment may be one cause.

The Interview

It's obvious, when considering the employer's and candidate's priorities as noted above, that the interview is a critical session in which a great deal of substantive information needs to be communicated by both parties. Unfortunately, few people have extensive interviewing experience and personnel or human resource professionals can be jaded by doing too much interviewing. Often what a person is saying and what they are thinking can differ vastly. However, the person who recognizes the variety of dynamics in play has an advantage and a better opportunity to get his or her message communicated as accurately as possible. Let's look at some methods to create the best platform of communication.

- Be prepared: Like the Boy Scout motto, always be prepared. Practice "due diligence." In business jargon this means make the effort to properly research the project. Research as much as you can about the firm before your interview. Find out who its clients are.

Preparation and Timing

Personal Style

Regional Styles

Find out what kind of work it specializes in (if any) and who is responsible for hiring. Find out who you will ultimately report to either before or during the interview. Recognize that the person interviewing you may only be able to make recommendations and not have the authority to hire you.

■ Additional portfolio material: Based on your information, you may want to bring along additional material pertinent to the company's needs, perhaps additional sketches. You might also consider bringing personal artwork (illustration, photography, etc.) and ask if the interviewer would like to see it. Be sure to offer this work as an optional consideration. Do not be put off if the interviewer doesn't have time or isn't interested.

■ Timing: Be punctual. Allow yourself some extra time if you're not sure how long it will take to get there. Check out your transportation options ahead of time, not at the last minute.

■ Attire: Dress in a professional manner. Every company has its own "culture" which dictates what is customary attire. Even if dress is very casual, you won't make a mistake by dressing for the interview. If you have only one interviewing suit, this is the time to wear it. When you are there you'll probably see how others dress and get a better idea of what it would be like for you inside the company. We knew one person who went to the office building a day or two before her interview and watched people leaving for lunch to see how they dressed. Another person we know took the subway on a hot New York day so as not to sit down and wrinkle her dress before an interview. She was meeting with a famous designer known for fashion and fragrance and knew her appearance was critical. This behavior is not silly or compulsive. It's smart.

The issue of "style" is the critical point. Style requirements can range from the high fashion image of a New York cosmetic firm to the conservative Midwestern corporation which believes a woman should not wear a pantsuit to an interview. It may seem unfair and perhaps sexist, but in today's world it is a fact of life. Style can mean the trendy New York or Los Angeles design studio whose dress code is based on Soho or Melrose Avenue. Style can also mean marketing communications firms and corporations that regard expensive, well-tailored suits with discreet accessories as the norm. Often I feel life is one big costume party and you have to decide which party you wish to attend. However, to deny the impact of these factors would be naive and ultimately close off opportunities. Lastly, the way you dress sends an important message to others in the same way good manners do. It says something about how you feel about your own image, possibly about the future you crave, and how you perceive the needs of your future employer.

The bottom line of this subject is that people really do lose jobs and opportunities based on their appearance and personal presentation. Be aware and be careful.

- Beginning: Conventional wisdom says that you have thirty seconds to make an impression. The way you say hello and shake hands says a great deal. Look people in the eye. The inability to sustain eye contact reveals personal insecurities or hidden agendas. I know at least two people who lost opportunities directly because of this factor. The employers expressed a feeling of "being uncomfortable" with someone who didn't offer direct eye contact. Some people, aware of the need for a firm, positive handshake as a sign of character, can nearly break one's hand. I always feel they have read some self-help book and taken it too much to heart. On the other hand (no pun intended) it's also surprising how many limp, damp handshakes I get. The bottom line is: Be yourself, be as relaxed as possible, and know that, nonetheless, someone is sizing you up instantly (and that person may be equally nervous). As a yoga practitioner, whenever I feel tense, I always try to breathe deeply, clear my mind of extraneous subjects as much as possible, and take heart in the fact that the person I'm going to meet is just another human being with many of the same insecurities as anyone. Be pleasant, respectful, and polite; ask where they would like you to sit, if it's not obvious. *Try to think of this person as a professional friend.* Think of yourself as being on the same side, as if you are already a part of his or her team and share the same objectives. Do not overstep your bounds.

First Impressions

Dynamics of Communication

Keeping Momentum

- Listening and responding: Let the person interviewing you take the lead and direct the conversation, at least in the beginning. There are likely to be plenty of opportunities for you to ask questions, *so practice the art of listening.* The ability to listen to another person and concentrate on what he or she is really saying (and sometimes what he or she thinks he or she is saying) is a very important trait. This is true not only in the interview, but throughout your business activities. Too often candidates are too intent on what they are going to say to listen to the interviewer. This may be because of nerves. If you listen carefully and address points the other person raises, your communication will be focused to that individual's criteria. You'll be able to direct your answers in a germane manner. It's surprising how few people know how to listen. We even get this quality listed as part of a job description. The request, "I want someone who knows how to listen," is not uncommon. If you're worried about remembering all your questions, bring along a written list. It's perfectly acceptable.

- Breaking appointments: Obviously this is something to avoid as it complicates situations and may send a negative message. In the first place, scheduling interviews can be a difficult task when it involves people with busy schedules who perhaps travel a great deal. Sometimes interviews are with more than one person and those schedules have to be coordinated. Changing appointments is acceptable when there is an understandable and, therefore, an acceptable reason. The risk is losing the "timing" or momentum of the opportunity. If it becomes a pattern, it can mean a loss of interest (perhaps for both parties). If you are not feeling well and not "up" for an interview, the best course is to postpone. Many interviews have been "blown" because the person was not functioning at full speed. If you decide to go to the meeting be sure to tell them why you are not up to par, that you didn't want to cancel and request to come back at another time.

- Confirming Appointments: Do it.

Classic Interview Questions

These are some common questions and topics you should be prepared to encounter. Every interviewer, naturally, has his or her own style of conducting an interview. Some are relaxed, some interrogatory. Remember, no matter how relaxed the atmosphere may be, it's a time for testing. Remember that your interview is really a time to assess your presentation skills. No matter how relaxed the environment may seem, you are still in a position of being judged. The yin and yang of the situation often hangs on the culture of the firm. People have not passed muster because they were too relaxed and informal (beware breakfast meetings on this one) and their presentation was not deemed "professional" enough or perhaps they were too "formal" in a firm that prides itself on being "young and loose." The key to these experiences is that the person and firm were probably not a fit, but one can't help wonder if errors in judgement were made.

- Why are you planning to leave your job and/or why are you interested in this firm? We have discussed many logical and appropriate reasons. Now is the time for you to be prepared to articulate them. Never, however, say anything negative or damaging about you last or current employer.
- Future goals: Be prepared for questions about how you perceive your future. This can be a dangerous trap. If you view this job as a temporary stage in your life, do not say so. The employer wants to know that if you are hired you will be there for a considerable and fair period of time. Understand that the first three to six months of your employment is probably going to involve a learning curve. The employer is investing in you and wants a reasonable return. We had one memorable time when a corporation flew a designer from coast to coast after initial interviews in his home city. Early on in the interview at corporate headquarters he was asked the famous and standard "personnel" question, "What is your five-year-goal?" His response was to have his own business. He was out the door soon after that answer, and the interviewer immediately picked up the phone to call me.
- Personal traits: Be prepared to answer questions that

attempt to identify your personal tastes and beliefs. Whom do you most admire? What has been a motivating force in your life? What books do you read? When was the last time you were in a museum? Where do you like to vacation? Questions that would be considered strictly personal (for example, intimate family details, such as plans to get married or have a baby, or about politics, sex, or age) are illegal. Therefore, these questions are designed to learn more about your personality and character. Employers are usually seeking a well-rounded individual with a variety of personal interests.

How to Show Motivation

- Motivation: Your personal motivation toward this position will be a key element in your interview. The entire manner of your participation in the interviewing process points to the level of your motivation, including your promptness, dress, etc. You need to articulate the level of your interest in the firm, job, and career opportunity, as well as the manner in which you are accustomed to working and your energy level. Basically you want to communicate to your future employer that you will welcome the opportunity to participate in the business, giving 110 percent of your talent, skills, energy, and ability.

- Lunch/Dinner/Drinks: Part of your interviewing process may include some time in a restaurant. There are several objectives to this kind of activity that are very important. They all relate to you as a thinking individual, to your manners, and how you conduct yourself publicly.
  1. While it is excellent to give both of you the chance for a less formal, relaxed meeting and to get to know each other, remember it is still part of the testing process. Knowing this, it is your task to show a relaxed, self-confident manner.

Manners and Mannerisms

  2. Being in a restaurant gives your future employer the opportunity to observe you in the surroundings in which business is often conducted. Your deportment, table manners, and level of sophistication would all impact on your relationships with your clients. How you make "small talk" and how you move on to the business issues are part of the game. If you happen to be ordering first, try not to order a

drink unless your host does. A majority of people today don't drink at lunch. You want to keep your wits about you anyway. Let your host be dominant, calling for the waiter, asking for the check. If you have checked your coats and are not paying for the meal it is proper for you to tip the coat room attendant.

- Questions to ask:

  1. Find out what is the organizational structure of the firm.
  2. Find out who you will report to and who will make the hiring decision. It may not be the same person who is conducting the interview.
  3. Ask if other interviews will be necessary and who you will be meeting with. Find out their titles so you'll understand their positions within the structure of the firm.
  4. Try to find out how long they have been looking for someone. If the job is open too long there may be a problem.
  5. Find out if it's a new position or a replacement. If it's a replacement it's always helpful to know why the person left; however, it may be a difficult question to ask. If it's a new position, carefully check out the expectation level regarding the job description. Often descriptions change on new positions because the employers may not have thought everything out thoroughly. New positions can often mean a better opportunity. It's also easier not to follow in another's footsteps.
  6. Ask when they plan to make a hiring decision and when they need someone to start. It is sometimes possible to find out how many people they are considering (giving you an idea of what the competition is like).
  7. Ask if you can see samples of their work. Remember what they do will go into your portfolio and affect your next position.

- Freelance and projects: Indicate you're available for freelance if it's possible for you to do so. Sometimes employers like to suggest a trial project as a test. If so, be sure to get as complete a briefing as possible of the nature of the project. You'll often be gauged against

How to Express Your Financial Needs

currently employed designers who may have the advantage of understanding the clients better. You should always be paid for any work you do. If you do work, ask if a purchase order is required so that you don't fall into "accounting limbo" and not get paid. If you do a project, make sure you deliver it on time.

- Salary: Toward the end of the interview you should ask what the firm is planning to pay for the position. However, you will probably be asked first what your salary expectations are. This may even come as a response to your question. Remember, salary is only a base. It must be viewed in the context of a whole package with benefits. This will be discussed in greater detail in chapter 12, The Money Question. For the purpose of this section, understand that it is an issue to be dealt with during the interview. This is always a difficult, sensitive moment if you don't have any prior information. Several options include:

  1. Telling your current salary and indicating you expect more (factors may include that you haven't been given an expected raise, the firm is having financial problems, you are up for a raise but you want to leave anyway for stated reasons).

  2. That money is not your reason for wanting this position and you'd feel better knowing how they evaluate your worth within their company.

  3. Indicating a range that you feel comfortable with, without using specific numbers, such as high twenties, low to mid thirties, etc.

  4. That this will be your first job and the opportunity is your foremost consideration (however, you still need to make a living). With regard to first jobs, please remember it's going to cost your employer to train you. You should always think of your first couple of positions as continuing education. Salaries are far less negotiable with corporations. You probably would be in discussion with a member of the human resources department who would be working with clear-cut schedules or guidelines.

- Concluding the interview: Make sure you understand the next phase of the interviewing process. Are you to get back in touch or will they contact you? Do they want any other materials from you? Do not fall into

Maintaining Continuity

the trap of calling them too often. The ball will be in their court and you have to take their lead. Sometimes firms are too polite, don't know how to say no, and may lead a person on unnecessarily. When you leave, say "Thank you." Get the person's business card if possible and send a thank you note if you're not coming back soon. Get the title and spelling correct on the note. If this is a position you are anxious to have, express that motivation in a note or letter. Tell the person responsible for hiring how much you want the job, why you believe you have much to offer, and how you would devote all your energies to the company. Strong motivation is a major factor in hiring decisions and you have nothing to lose by assuming an aggressive stance.

Confidentiality and Non-Compete Agreements

You may be asked to sign a letter or contract relating to the proprietary business of the firm. It could also involve non-compete agreements should you leave the firm. The purpose of most confidentiality and non-compete agreements are to prevent you from (1) discussing any proprietary information, (2) contacting or soliciting business from their clients, and (3) soliciting their employees for a defined period of time (a specific number of months or years) after your employment has been terminated (usually for any reason). Just understand that this is common practice among many design firms and the number of firms attempting to restrict departing employees is on the rise. While there are many terms of these agreements that are completely legal, it is not legal to restrict anyone form earning a living in his or her chosen profession. Therefore the language of these agreements is critical, since the structure of these contracts can vary greatly, and laws can vary from state to state. *It is absolutely necessary not to sign anything without first showing it to an attorney* , as signing the wrong agreement could hamper your future ability to be employed.

Psychological Testing

There are many types of tests to qualify different kinds of information. A small percentage of corporations use these devices. Your decision to accept taking the test is strictly voluntary, but may be a condition attached to getting the job.

Medical Examinations

Passing a medical exam is a reasonably common require-ment for corporations but not consultant firms. It may also be necessary if there is an insurance policy attached to the benefits package. The last few years have seen a rise in drug and HIV testing as well. It is possible you may be asked for a blood or urine sample. Several Wall Street firms we know will "spring" a urine test on an applicant during one of the interviewing appointments without forewarning. These tests can pick up traces of marijuana or a poppy seed bagel di-gested three days before the test. Needless to say you won't be penalized for eating bagels but we advise people to be aware of what they are ingesting if they know they're due for a test.

References

You should always be ready to offer references, if re-quested. If you have letters of reference, bring them to the interview. You can ask the interviewer if he or she would like to have a copy, but it may or may not be necessary. Refer-ences are generally requested in the last stage of candidate selection just before an offer is extended. At that time it is common practice to present three references. Usually, if you are is still employed, it is not possible to get a reference from your current employer. In that case, seek references from a confidant in your office or someone you reported to at an-other office. Other likely references would be people whom you supervised, those whom you dealt with as vendors (photographers, illustrators, suppliers), and anyone else who could speak about your ability to follow instructions, super-vise others, meet deadlines, hold to budgets, and the like. References should be as recent as possible and no more than three to four years past. When your future employer is calling your references personally, be sure to allow time for you to alert them to expect the call (and double-check that they are available).

Accepting or Rejecting an Offer

Accepting an offer is a fairly uncomplicated affair. If you are not presently working, you need only find out when the firm wishes you to start. Perhaps first you'll need to fulfill a freelance obligation. Remember though, if you have any work obligations, finishing them is professionally correct no matter how much pressure is placed on you by your new employer. Never walk away from a promise. Your future employer wouldn't want you to do it to him or her either, and perhaps she or he may need that as a reminder. For some reason, once employers have made up their minds to hire they often want the instant gratification of having the employee on premises immediately. If you have to leave a position, you'll have to do so in the same professional manner in which you conduct all your business dealings. We'll cover that subject in some detail in chapter 13, Moving On—When and How to Leave a Job.

Rejecting an offer is a matter of diplomacy. Your reasons for rejecting a position can be many and show an exercise of sound judgement. However, it's important to remember that an employer faces your rejection with about the same distaste as you would feel being rejected by a firm you wanted to join. As always, it's important to consider how it is for the other person. The employer has made a decision based on the whole hiring procedure. Perhaps it was very time-consuming. He or she now has to start all over again. Significantly, you may want to "leave the door open" for future opportunities with that firm, or simply understand that as individuals who move about in an industry, you may meet again. The effect is the same. You need to reject the offer with grace and professionalism. Thank them for the opportunity the offer represents and give a reasonably clear understanding of why you are not accepting. Do not in any way insult them or their firm with your rejection. If you don't like their work, find another reason. Only raise the issue of insufficient salary if you would accept the job for more money, for they may come up with a

A Matter of Diplomacy

better offer. Tell them the truth if you have another offer you feel is superior. The reason (such as working conditions, growth opportunity, benefit package) may be constructive. Just keep in mind that you may meet again.

Summary   In summary, let's consider the whole picture of the hiring process. Your portfolio is the access to the firm, the foot in the door to determine whether your creative point of view and talent are appropriate to the firm's business core. The next stage in this process centers around you as a person. All the criteria listed really focus on what you are about. Your personality, attitude, upbringing, and goals come into play as critical components. The last phase relates to whether you determine this position is the right direction for the long term. If the firm is of like mind, it will make an offer. I've referred to the synergistic relationship between employee and employer as a dance for two. It is a partnership of the first order of importance. Every combination of personalities is unique in every sense of the word. Situations are never quite duplicate. (That is what makes my work so fascinating.) I always advise, when the decision to accept or reject is most difficult, *to listen to that small voice within you.* Sometimes it's just a "feeling" in the pit of your stomach. Contemplate, listen, but don't fear risk. Nothing is achieved without it. ■

12

The Money Question

Salary negotiations are probably among the most difficult matters for the average person. Compounding the issue is the knowledge that these negotiations are essential and an extremely distasteful process to be avoided if at all possible. And because it's so subjective, most designers practice avoidance, diminishing their earning capability. The negotiating process with its resulting salary package is, of course, the integral ingredient of any employment contract. Negotiation is an art form not taught as part of any design curriculum. In addition, we are again confronted with the issue of choice. How can you negotiate if you don't know what the possibilities and choices are?

Salary Variables: What Are You Worth?

You are in an interview, you really want the position, and you are asked what your salary requirements are. How do you respond? It is always easier to be passive and respond to a number offered, but the blatant act of firmly stating a number you want is often very difficult. Perhaps it's the whole issue of assigning a number as an indication of one's worth. It's putting a price on your head. Are you secure and forthright or do you hedge, knowing that you'll take any reasonable offer?

How do you establish your worth as a creative person? How do you price creativity? Financial ignorance plays an important role in this process because many designers simply don't know what they are worth in the marketplace or what the market will bear. This information is hard to come by.

Surveys The only gauges are occasional salary surveys like the ones published by the AIGA (American Institute of Graphic Arts), The Industrial Designers Society of America Compensation Study, The Design Management Institute, or The Graphic Artist's Guild. To inquire about the most recent surveys contact these organizations directly. Full contact information is listed in the appendix.

Newspaper ads and trade publications are also a market-wise indication of current salary offerings; however, many ads use the ambiguous phrase "salary is competitive and commensurate with experience." It certainly leaves the person applying for that job at a disadvantage. Some salary information is hearsay or of the classic "grapevine" variety.

"Street-Wise" Information Within a few companies there is often a "feeling" or underground knowledge by the staff of how much various employees earn. But more often, especially in a larger firm, individuals are operating in the dark with little knowledge of what their colleagues or counterparts earn. Friends are little help, for few want to confide how much they earn.

Employers usually assume one of two opposing positions regarding releasing income information. One is to create parity between employees (probably recognizing as well that eventually there are few secrets in firms), the other is that all financially related information is proprietary and strictly confidential.

Employees sometimes embark on job searches just to learn what they can earn by making a move, and use that information to negotiate an increase with their employers. I

Counteroffers have always felt that is a form of blackmail and I wouldn't be happy staying with a firm who would only acknowledge my real worth at the equivalent of gunpoint. It's my opinion that the employee is never perceived the same way again, by the employer or by his or her colleagues in the workplace, who usually end up knowing the whole story. Counteroffers are reasonably common, however, and some feel it's a better course of action than making a move to another firm and therefore into the unknown. It becomes a matter of personal business philosophy and must be dealt with on a case-by-case basis. Also, there are many firms that will, on principle, never make a counteroffer.

What is the best way to overcome this lack of information and find a reasonable path toward salary equity? Once again, the responsibility for the research effort falls on the designer's shoulders. If you want a realistic picture, it is necessary to utilize the above-mentioned sources and try to make a personal survey. Professional recruiters, like those at my firm, are probably one of these best sources for this confidential information. In fact, our firm is such an excellent barometer of the marketplace and of salaries around the country that we are often asked to advise our clients on what they need to pay. In some instances we work as consultants to design firms and corporations who need our expertise on comparative and equitable compensation scales. In addition we have developed a survey which we distribute at various speaking engagements. You will find that survey at the end of this chapter. Some contributing factors in gauging salaries are:

Reality Check

Contributing Factors

- Regional: Questions of location are very important. The cost of living and cost of overhead will influence pay scales. There are distinct differences in salary levels in New York, Los Angeles, Atlanta, or Seattle.
- Economic: Salaries can reflect a buyer's or seller's market. Wages will be affected by recessions. Then there are regional factors. The boom and then dry periods Texas has experienced through the 1980s and 1990s would be an excellent example.
- Size: Small firms generally have smaller budgets if smaller companies comprise their client base. Size of the firm is only meaningful when considered in relation to its client base. There are many small firms (under twenty people) who have high-profile clients and therefore command parity in fees with large firms.
- The type of firm: Studios and marketing communications firms may not have the same budgets as large corporations, but it is difficult to generalize because there are exceptions for every rule. One must consider that the major differences between corporate and non-corporate positions are in the areas of benefits and

freedom to negotiate. Corporate benefits are usually far more expansive (see Benefits Packages) than a private firm can offer. Corporate salaries are another matter. They are usually formulated on a sliding scale set to gauge levels of experience and the quality of responsibility defined in the job description. Corporate salaries will thus be graded and pegged to titles with a high and low range. Corporations like to hire at the low-to-medium range, leaving room for salary increases through the years of employment. Should the individual reach the top of the range, his or her only recourse to future salary growth would be a change in job description and title. With such firm guidelines it is easy to understand that negotiating a salary with a corporation is far more restrictive than negotiating with a group based on an entrepreneurial business mode.

■ Supply and Demand: As in any marketplace these factors can easily effect pricing. Recessions and booms will have the obvious effect, and yet, as I write this in 1996, we are experiencing another phenomenon: the lack of qualified talent. For the last couple of years there are more positions open than qualified people to fill them. The hiring criteria falls into the patterns described in this book, but the resulting frustrations in acquiring talent has pushed the salaries upwards, translating into higher compensation packages.

■ Specialization: Different areas of business command higher fees. Two extreme examples would be feature films and book design. The entertainment field offers much higher compensation than book publishing. Since creative people are often driven by what they enjoy doing in contrast to where the most money can be earned, this information will be more important to some than to others. However, it is at least important to understand what the possibilities can be when making life choices. The Salary Survey at the end of this chapter points out some of the differentials.

What's Your Job Worth?

A controlling element in setting salaries is the amount of business particular design projects can generate. The greater the financial impact of the product and its ability to encourage sales, the greater the financial rewards. With that principle clarified it's easy to understand why an advertising creative director can realize a salary of perhaps a quarter-to-a-half million dollars, which is far more that any designer would hope for. Consider the amount of money at stake in the placement of a television commercial scheduled to air during a Super Bowl or Olympic's broadcast. Consider the cost of airing the commercial, the cost of production in making it, and the financial and image risk to the corporate sponsor. With all that at stake, is any one going to quibble about how much it will cost to hire the best talent?

The higher the stakes for image and sales, the larger the compensation for doing the job right. It's easy to understand. As we have discussed, within the design field we have companies which have various specialities. The associated expertise contributes to set the value of the services. Specialists are experts who will be compensated more than generalists. A comparison to health care is not unfounded. A general practitioner will usually charge less for an office visit than a specialist. Design firms or agencies creating movie advertising, title treatments, and trailers find themselves in a particularly richly compensated, if volatile, area. Firms specializing in identity, whether corporate, branding, or retail, are at the higher end of the compensation scale. After all, how often is a corporation going to change its identity? Think of the impact of that new system. Packaging design can also hold great importance as it directly contributes to sales at the point of sale. Book design, while hardly insignificant, has the least effect, as most people will buy a book for reasons other than its appearance (thus, they don't judge a book by its cover). Editorial designers have direct impact on a magazines' image and sales. One look at a newsstand, with all those covers screaming for your attention, will confirm that the magazines' appearance contributes to the message "buy me!" The interior spreads continue to reinforce the magazines' content, message, and legibility.

Benefit Packages

Many benefits and perks are available, and can drastically change from one firm to another. The best option is to know what could possibly be available versus what the standard package is for a company. Then see if there is any room to negotiate. A large corporation with a rather complete package may indeed offer most items while small design firm may offer just a few. The following is not a complete listing, but will give you an idea of some of the potential opportunities to add to compensation.

- Health Insurance: This has become the most costly area for employers. The explosion in health insurance costs over the past few years has, in many cases, required employers to seek other methods of coverage. HMOs or organized health plans offering a selected group of physicians have gained in popularity. Many firms have raised the deductible base and/or have made their plans contributory. This means that the employee must assume some of the costs. The percentages vary from firm to firm. While some form of medical insurance is standard practice for most offices, dental insurance is not as commonly available. Most medical plans cover psychiatric treatments (or sessions) in a modest way, but do not give it the same benefit scale as other physicians. However, one of this country's top corporations operates a sanitorium exclusively for its employees. (Perhaps this is an interesting message about the cost of "making it" in America.)

- Health Clubs: In recognition of the long-term benefits of a healthy employee, many large corporations will have on-site health clubs or gyms. Some firms will offer memberships in commercial health club facilities. For some senior individuals a country club membership is a negotiable point.

- Vacations, Holidays, Personal, and Sick Days: This category is self-explanatory and can vary from one firm to another to a great extent. The ability to "buy" an additional week of vacation is a newer option offered by some firms. "Buying" can mean approved leave without pay or earning "time credits" with unused sick day allowances.

- Leave of Absence: This can be negotiated on a case-by-case basis. Most firms do not have specific policies in place.

- Life and Disability Insurance: Most major medical policies include a life insurance plan equal to one year's income. Senior level personnel can often negotiate an increased life insurance benefit, as well as disability insurance.

- Expense Accounts: Travel and entertainment expenses that are directly related to the firm's business are paid directly or reimbursed by the company. It is possible to be given a guaranteed annual amount as a perk. However, all such expenditures have to be documented with receipts.

- Company Transportation: Many firms will offer a company car to senior level employees. Often it is a negotiable item and the make of the car becomes a status symbol, recognizing the seniority of the employee. Sometimes the negotiation surrounding the make of car can be tense, for the significance lies in the message sent to the rest of the firm regarding the person's status.

  Monthly auto rentals can also be part of the package when a firm needs an employee to travel as part of the job. It can also be a factor if the firm is in a fairly inaccessible location for the employee they wish to hire. Company vans, buses, and airplanes are occasionally available as necessary.

- Commutation: If the office location is considered an lengthy distance to commute, the firm may offer to pay these expenses.

- Pension Plans: There are several plans available, all of which operate on the same principle of placing money into holding accounts for retirement before paying taxes on those funds. Common plans are the 401k and SEP-IRA. These plans can be payroll deductions, employer's contributions, or a combination of contributions by the employees and employers. Some plans stipulate a period of time to become vested. This means you cannot be eligible to receive the funds unless you stay with the firm for a specific number of years. There may be a sliding scale of eligibility. For example, after five years of employment a 50 percent; vestment after six years 60 percent; etc. The advantage of all these plans, regardless of your age, is that they become a form of forced savings and/or additional monies to your base salary that are not taxable. They work as the common IRA. The money accrued in the plan is not taxable until you receive it.

- Education: Some firms offer continued education benefits, reimbursing you for all or part of your expenses. Most plans will only cover educational programs germane to your profession. Some plans will have coverage for family members.

- Seminars and Conferences: Since these are also considered to be educational, many firms, on request, will pay these expenses. They have added value as vehicles for making new contacts for the firm and as a general internal public relations effort.

- Company Stock: Stock or stock options are available on a case-by-case basis. Keep in mind there are many ways of offering stock and many grades of stock. Stock, as well as profit-sharing, is used as a form of equity in the firm.

- Profit-Sharing: Some firms distribute a percentage of their profits to employees as an incentive. The incentive is to have a vested interest in the general welfare of the company and contribute to its profitability. Obviously the numbers will change from year to year but the system is an excellent method of insuring the employee's role within the company.

- Bonuses: The bonus is totally optional. It can be a year-end or semiannual disbursement based on performance and profitability. Remember, since it is a cash award, the money is completely taxable. In addition to the "reward" system bonus, some firms can offer a sign-on bonus as an incentive to attract an individual. For the firm it means a one-time additional charge without changing the salary base.

- Relocation: Most corporations will include a relocation package for individuals who will move to the site of the company. This is most prevalent with companies which are located in cities where there is an insufficient talent pool. However, that does not mean a company will not pay relocation expenses from one major city to another. The obvious fact is no company wants to incur extra expenses, but if the individual has the unique requirements needed, the money will be there. For smaller firms, paying the price of a move is often out of the question. It should be clear that a smaller company will only pay these costs for experienced personnel. Corporations will relocate a junior-level designer when they recruit from art schools. If a person of only a few years' experience wishes to be in a certain geographical region, the best strategy would be to research the firms in the area, perhaps by calling the local chapter of the AIGA (the American Institute of Graphic Arts) or Art Directors Club. Get listings of member firms, contact them directly, and, ultimately, travel to seek the position and be prepared to move yourself. When visiting a new city, give yourself enough time, perhaps even allowing time to freelance. It is always frustrating for me to see designers come to New York for ten days or two weeks and expect to return home with a job offer. Relocation costs most often include air fare (with perhaps a couple of visits to find a home), the cost of bringing a spouse to see the new city, and actual moving expenses for belongings. It can also include (but not always) temporary residence, expenses, furniture storage costs, help finding schools, day care, even a job for the spouse, help with mortgage points, and sometimes assuming the mortgage and sale of the previous home. Sometimes a flat package is offered to cover these costs and sometimes a smaller firm can offer to pay part of the expenses. Remember, in these cases, you must always be able to document your expenses with receipts.

- Child Care/Elder Care: Unfortunately, very few firms offer on-site care or any allowance to pay for outside facilities. The only firms that have moved in this direction are large corporations.
- Flex Time/Job Sharing: While very few firms are actively involved in flex time or job sharing, the concept to accommodate working parents is gaining momentum. Flex time is defined as the right not to work the standard nine to five and to establish hours that are responsive to the needs of working parents. Perhaps there is a need to work a shorter day but to be able to do some work at home. Several firms in New York have given young mothers a computer and mo-

dem to work at home and communicate with the studio electronically. This networking capability is adding a new dimension to defining the workplace. Job sharing is another option. Two people share one job, usually overlapping one day to insure a communications flow. Since graphic design is comprised of a vast female majority (and the numbers are growing every year), the ability to control work time individually will without doubt grow in response to the need.

- Mommy-Track Part-Time Employment: This has become a viable option for some companies. It allows them to access talent and control budgets, and offers, for some mothers, the best of both worlds.

- Employee Handbooks: Most large companies and many small ones have their benefits and policies spelled out in some form of printed material. You should always ask for it. It is a clear indication of what you can expect as the basis of the firm's offerings. However, many of the items listed above can become negotiable points in the hiring procedure. I have indicated the most common areas. It's always helpful to know what's possible. Keep in mind, however, that many perks are not available to junior employees. There is a clear correlation between the perception of value associated with the employee and the amount of rewards a company will offer.

Negotiating a Salary

Again, the advantage is with the person who can view the process in a holistic way, understanding the various economic forces at work. Taking a job and negotiating a salary is a complex endeavor and many facets of the opportunity must be weighed against each other. These considerations should include:

- The nature of the position
- The long- or short-term goals of the designer
- The quality of the firm and its business agenda
- The areas of specialization (if any)
- Market factors
- Location
- Benefits

Benefit packages, as described above, are extremely important because they represent non-cash or cash-deferred additions to your salary that are equivalent to cash value based on *after-tax dollars*. This means that the cash value is more that its face value because it is non-taxable income.

The actual negotiation can be informal, friendly, and brief. A scenario can be a casual—"This is what we feel we can offer you"—and, since the amount is not a surprise and is agreeable, you accept. Other offers can be far more formal and in a "testing" mode. The quality of the negotiation can establish the power relationships that will continue on the job. This is a time in which you want to be sure to conduct yourself in a cautious and professional manner. Be respectful and courteous, no matter what you may think. It is a general rule of thumb to ask for a little more than you expect to get. If you feel there is room to negotiate, on principal, don't accept a first offer.

A far more common scenario to the one above would be not to respond immediately after you receive a offer, but to defer your response a few days. Give yourself time to "sleep on it." This will give you the opportunity to ponder and gain some clarity. Make sure you know all the other factors in addition to base salary when you get the offer. If there is some part of the offer that is not satisfactory, bring it up.

Salary Reviews

The timing of salary reviews can become an important issue in discussions of this nature. The first stage is to have the firm specify their review policy and its definition. A review usually means an evaluation of work performance and a possible change in compensation based on the review. It can take place at year end or at the anniversary of the employee joining the firm. Sometimes it can take place much earlier. If the amount offered is deemed insufficient you may ask for an earlier review, perhaps within three or six months. We have found this a generally excellent method to negotiate a higher salary with a time limit for the lower salary. The amount of the future increase is usually not determined at the time of hiring, but the review agreement represents an understanding that an increase is possible at a specific time if performance matches expectation. It also affords the employer less risk if the quality of the employee's work and experience is in question.

The number of items to be negotiated can sometimes be a surprise. The old adage "everything in life is negotiable" may

1996 SALARY SURVEY

for annual starting salaries shown in thousands

FIELD	ENTRY LEVEL Junior	5 YEARS EXPERIENCE Intermediate	10+ YEARS EXPERIENCE Senior
Identity / Branding			
Packaging Design	$28–32	$35–45	senior designers $50–65 project directors: $55–70
Brand & Corporate	"	"	design directors: $75+
Identity Design	"	"	creative directors: $90–175+
Environmental Designers	"	"	
Product Designers	"	"	
Print Design			
Annual Reports	$25–35	$35–50	senior designers $50–65 design directors: $65–80
Corporate Literature	"	"	creative directors: $75–100+
Editorial			
Assistant Art Directors	$30–35		
Associate Art Directors		$35–40	
Art Directors		$40–75	
Art Directors/Senior Art Directors/Design Directors			$80–130 +
Corporations			
Asst Art Directors/Designers	$30–35	$35–50	
Art Directors			$55–80
Design Managers		$40–60	$55–80
Design Directors			$65–90
Creative Directors			$75–150
V.P. Creative Director/Creative Services			$85–350+
Account Management (Marketing Communications/Design)			
Project Managers	$35–50	$40–60	
Account Services	"	"	
Account Executives		$50–75	$65–100
Senior Consultants			$100–150+
Marketing/Sales	$30–40	$40–60	$75–175+

Advertising Agencies

General Advertising

Art Directors/Copy Writers	$25–35	$45–60	$65–85
Associate Creative Directors			$100–150
TV Stars (Art Directors with major commercial credits)			$200 +

Sales Promotion

Art Directors/Copy Writers	$22–27	$50–60	$60–70
Associate Creative Directors			$75–90
Creative Directors			$100–200 +

TV Production

Line Producer	$50–90	
Production Supervisor		$100–125

Interactive Media

Designers	$30–40	$40–60	
Art Directors		$50–65	$60–85
Design Directors (small-to-midsize firms)			$85–130
Design Directors (Advertising Agencies)			$90–150
Vice President/ Design Director			$120–185
Web Masters		$30–40	$50–70
Programmers		$60–80	
Tech Directors			$80–120

Production

Advertising/Print	$25–28	$40–50	$60–100+
Annual Reports	"	"	$60–85+
Packaging	"	$40–60	$75–100+

Regional Factors

Los Angeles/San Francisco: 10% less

MidWest/South/NorthWest: at least 15% less

Note: + means package of perks that significantly changes compensation not be completely true, but is a helpful motto. As long as you do not have an arrogant attitude, your loss exposure in trying to change terms is negligible and you have everything to gain. However, I would caution you that in any negotiation, you must concentrate on realistic priorities. For example, it would be futile for a designer with two years experience to negotiate a four-week vacation when the standard is two weeks.

Corporations and many firms may confirm the agreement with a written offer stating the terms. Smaller firms may consider a handshake sufficient. Nonetheless, make sure your offer is real and confirmed and not in an exploratory phase. Every now and then we find a designer who believes he or she has a job offer when the employer is really trying to determine if he or she is available at a certain salary. The confusion is easily understandable, but you would not want to quit a job based on an incomplete offer.

To sum it up, salary packages are always flexible, an ever-shifting set of priorities and goals. The possible combinations of all these components make for a tremendous variety of possibilities. Establishing a package that's fair and equitable to both parties depends heavily upon what both perceive as fair. Designers are unique in that accepting positions often has little to do with the salary and a great deal to do with the quality of work, the quality of opportunity, and general lifestyle it offers. Perhaps the best advice is to always go with your basic instinct of what is comfortable for you. The bottom line is always an extremely subjective one. ■

13

Moving On: When and How to Leave a Job

It's time." That is the most common response I get when I ask an applicant why they want to look for another job. What does this internal clock signal? What are the signs that mark the moment to embark on such a career-altering process? Most often it means there is "no place to go." This often-used phrase means that the path forward and upward is blocked. It may be blocked by another person who occupies the position you want and that person shows no indication of leaving or being promoted. It may mean the size of the firm and its structure will not allow for a logical progression. It may mean that if you stay in the safety of your present position without being promoted you will stop growing professionally. "No place to go" often means "no place to grow." It's a feeling of reaching a plateau and not being willing to stay there.

No Place to Go Means No Place to Grow

As design matures and changes over any given period of years there is, for some, a sense that their firms may not have kept pace with the times. Companies who have not set their sights forward find themselves in a perilous trap. They fail to keep up with the marketing trends or computerization, and the result is often a creative brain drain. The employee's sense of frustration and the desire to be current will cause many individuals to recognize that the only way they will achieve a state of competitive professionalism is to change their jobs.

Now, not everyone wants to constantly move up and that's fine. Many reach a position of contentment and comfort and stay in a firm for many years. But for the younger person still carving out a future from a collection of experiences, or for the person whose ambition is frustrated, "it's time" has a powerful ring.

Nonetheless, other reasons exist for making a move. Money can often be a very compelling cause. Supporting a family, buying a home, and other personal motivations may cause dissatisfaction with the present work condition. Professional growth being thwarted or not rewarded inspires the need to change. A glance at the "frustrations" list in chapter 11, The Candidate's Viewpoint, will identify and confirm the many root causes launching the decision to move on. Work environment, lack of recognition, and the desire to move to another city, can all be factors.

How to Quit

For some reason, we are often told how to educate ourselves, how to get a job, how to work, how to design, but little is ever said about how to quit. Acting in a responsible and professional manner once you have decided to leave is just as important as your demeanor when entering a new office. How you leave and the impression you make will affect your relationships with the people involved for the rest of your life. And don't think that once you have left a place you have closed that chapter of your life and it's finished. We have discussed how "round" the world is and how closely people keep interacting with each other through the years. There are constant reminders in everyday conversations of how people seem always amazed to meet up with the past. The key factor is never "burn bridges." It doesn't matter whether you are motivated by a desire to be considered a pleasant and likeable person or because you have the aspiration to maintain your people network. You should never block your access to anyone you might want to see again or have to be with again.

Maintaining your credibility and your professional relationships will strongly affect your performance in the workplace and your ability for future networking. There is nothing less productive than to leave a bad impression, or leave a place without grace and then find the same individuals working in the same firm with you years later. It happens! It happens with such frequency it pushes the point of plausibility.

You never know when you will need a recommendation, help of any sort, or perhaps even a job from individuals known through previous employment. The bottom line is paths keep crossing. We have witnessed these scenarios often in this game of professional musical chairs.

Let's consider a few amusing and sometimes not amusing examples. There was the young designer who left a firm with great hostility and anger. She left in a huff, telling her supervisor exactly what she thought of him! (How many times did you only wish for such an opportunity?) You probably can guess the rest of the story. Two jobs later that same supervisor was hired as a creative director in her firm. It was a very uncomfortable situation, saved only by his understanding that people can make mistakes. One person was hired for a three-month, temporary position. The employer went out of his way to make an easy transition after the three months by having the person work part-time while looking for another position. As it was also over the Christmas holidays, the employee was still given presents and a small bonus. When the person left she informed the office manager of her last day, but never said one word to the employer, let alone a good-bye. How could she expect a good reference?

Knowing how to say good-bye is as important as saying hello. It is critical to say "thank you." You should say thank you for having the opportunity to work and grow, to learn, to partake of whatever the success of the firm represented, to have accepted any gratuities that were given to you, any time that was spent on your behalf, and any effort the firm made to train you and allow you to reach the point where you could leave. Firms often recognize when "it's time" as well as you do, and do not experience any animosity at your departure. Many times individuals are anxious and perhaps frightened over the imagined confrontation in the act of resigning. The result can be a relief or letdown, and even a humbling experience, to learn that it may not be a big deal. Experienced and seasoned employers acknowledge the natural

Maintaining Relationships

How to Say Good-bye

process of moving on. Your resignation may cause them some disappointment, but, without question, they will find a method of replacing you. Leaving a job is another time when you must exhibit your sophistication and show professional manners and polish. Remember, whatever you may really be thinking is not the issue.

This is also a point in time to understand you may have an employer who truly does not want you to leave and may make a counteroffer. It is a time to keep clear focus on your reasons for leaving. If they are purely monetary, the counter-offer may have a significance to you. However, remember that few people leave a firm only for reasons of money. Chances are that nothing fundamentally changes in most established organizations as people/business patterns are well estab-lished, so beware of promises that cannot be kept. I do not find counteroffers flattering or wise in the vast majority of instances. Consider, if your value to the firm is that much greater, why did it take this action for you to get an increase?

And If You're Fired?

Let's face it—it can happen. Recessions and company restructuring have afforded too many people just that un-pleasant experience. The first half of the 1990s produced huge lay-offs due to corporate down-sizing and merger activity, as well as design firms restructuring to meet new electronic staffing requirements. It was estimated, in a study conducted by the *New York Times,* that one-third of middle management positions in corporations disappeared during the years—dramatically, and perhaps forever, changing the staffing profiles of these companies. Many euphemisms have come into the vernacular to try to alleviate the negative emotions attached to the words "fired." Some are kind, others represent corporate-speak that can be dehumanizing. We experience a broad range of explanations of this action. Almost no one ever says "You're fired!" However, whether you have been let go, cut back, re-structured, excessed, or re-engineered, the effect is exactly the same.

Unless you were let go for a reason, there is little stigma attached to being fired. The process of firms paring down has become all too common and acceptable. Other causes may be the lack of sufficient capitalization for many design firms, especially for start-up companies or new divisions of existing companies associated with the fast-moving and developing world of new media. Often if a client is lost, cash flow is immediately threatened, as the firm may not have a sufficiently broad or established client base. Agencies can have "Black Fridays" when a major account leaves, forcing them to immediately fire large numbers of people. Corporations, traditionally the slowest to react to a slowdown in revenues, will usually first seek to cut staff by attrition. However, as previously noted, they are no longer the bastions of employment security and are constantly subject to mergers and/or selling off divisions. The bottom line is, when interviewing, simply tell the truth.

If you were let go for reasons relating to performance, you have a significantly different problem. If you have fallen prey to internal political fall-out, you will have to be very tactful in how you describe the situation to a future employer. But, in either case, it is essential that you present a logical reason for your dismissal. Most often we are confronted with explanations referring to a "difference of opinion" or "creative conflict" or simply company politics. Whenever you are faced with a problem of describing internal company conflicts be very general; and beware of offering any libelous information. Remember, whatever you think about the organization you wish to leave or have left should not be reviewed in detail with future employers. If you have had negative experiences or observed business practices of which you don't approve, it is wise to keep it to yourself. If you are asked why you wish to leave or have left a position, choose your words carefully. You could be inviting legal action by libeling another person or company.

If you feel you were wrongfully fired and you wish to protest in some manner, do not sign anything during your exit interview. If you are presented with any documents, show it to an attorney first. Your attorney may also advise you not to accept any severance pay.

Severance pay is often a way of compensating an individual who has been let go. Severance is not mandatory and the amount varies greatly from firm to firm. Most of the time it is based on the number of years you have been a member of the firm, and many firms indicate the rules of severance pay in employee handbooks. Nonetheless, if you are not sure, always ask if you are entitled to severance pay or whether

Defining the Reason

Severance

the firm would like to consider giving it to you. Often this can be a negotiable item.

Finishing Work in Progress

Leaving also means not leaving unfinished work or leaving the firm with a problem on its hands. You must be conscientious and professional about your assignments and responsibilities. Sometimes you may be pressured by the firm you are joining to come on board as quickly as possible. You may be the end product of a long search and you represent needed relief in the workplace. The firm's deadlines are its main priority. The proper notice of leaving is at least two weeks. (In Europe it can mean one to three months.) The amount of notice you give your employer can be more or less dependent on work loads and the length of time you have been with the firm. If you have been there less than a year, one week is acceptable. Do not allow pressure to prevent you from finishing your work and/or handing it over to a co-worker. Your new employer wouldn't want you to leave him or her in a lurch either. Nonetheless, know that at some point it is important not to drag out the process through a misguided sense of responsibility. You have a responsibility to your new employer and to your future.

We had one unusual example when an employer insisted the individual report immediately to work or lose the job offer. He needed her to join immediately a team on a business trip to Japan. He recognized that if she was not part of the original team, the Japanese would never fully accept her. She was, however, in the middle of a project that she did not feel should be left suddenly. The job offer was about to be rescinded when we were finally able to negotiate a compromise. She went to Japan for two weeks and upon her return finished the other project while working for her new employer part-time.

Obtaining Portfolio Samples

Industry practice dictates you should have access to samples of all your work, including projects in which you have participated. It is your responsibility to present your work accurately, indicating the level of your responsibility, especially if the project was a shared one. Before and when you leave a firm you are entitled to samples of your work for your portfolio, barring confidentiality restrictions if products have not yet been released to the public. Some employers can make it difficult, and while there are no legal regulations per se (with the exception of proprietary or confidential projects), common past business practice indicates your entitlement to examples of your past experiences.

Upon exiting a firm, therefore, there may be recent samples you should be sure to request. You probably had updated your portfolio in order to seek employment, but don't forget to collect your most current samples. Perhaps it's new work that's at the printer and you will have to return in order to get it. You may have been working on sensitive projects that cannot be released until they are marketed. Make sure you get them later. These details are easily forgotten in the excitement of change and often are only remembered when you next seek a job and realize you require them for your book. By then it's probably too late. Always protect yourself by keeping an archive of your work history (with duplicates), including your ideation sketches, up to date. The work that most often gets left behind or simply discarded are the preliminary sketches. It is these sketches that are a key component of your portfolio. (See chapter 10, Your Portfolio.)

Exit Interviews

A segment of the departing process may be an "exit interview." It may be with a human resource person or with your boss. It should be a time of reflection and constructive evaluation. It may include a written questionnaire. The purpose is two-fold. First, it will give you tools in your search for a new job (if you are being let go) and second, it will allow you to evaluate the company from your point of view. If handled properly, it should give the firm an insight into its dealings with employees.

References

It is a very good idea to ask for a letter of reference upon departure. If you are leaving for another position, you may feel it's a moot point. It's a legitimate request in any case and may turn out to be handy for the future.

Vacations

The luxury of a vacation, be it short or long, between jobs is a terrific advantage. The physical and psychological breather refreshes your outlook and revitalizes your energy level. Of course, not everybody can take advantage of this possibility, but consider it an option. Every vacation day you can squeeze into your demanding schedule is a boon.

Some individuals prefer to quit after a vacation period or after a bonus period. This is manipulative but not surprising behavior. It is always questionable to me. If you want to factor in these often deserved and earned benefits then do so, but don't quit immediately, at least for appearance's sake.

Giving Notice

While you may want to give the customary two weeks notice, in some cases quitting may mean you'll leave before the day is out. In some business sectors you will probably be asked to leave the office the minute you give notice. This is mostly due to the confidential nature of the projects. The proprietary nature of the work takes precedence over time considerations. It's particularly true in branding and packaging design. The sensitivity of the projects has to be protected immediately, especially if the designer is moving to a competitor. In that case, the two weeks' notice is forgotten, and you will be wished good luck and told to pack up and leave. For the uninitiated it can be a rude shock. It is wise to be emotionally and professionally prepared for this possibility. However, this release can offer you a forced vacation, or you may find yourself starting your new position sooner than expected.

After you have left, be careful not to discuss your former employer's confidential projects. If you signed a confidentiality agreement, read it again carefully. Make sure you adhere to its restrictions. Whether you signed an agreement or not, the work you did at your previous firm is considered confidential, as are the work procedures. Keep in mind that certain knowledge is proprietary and you must not abuse that responsibility. If you do so, in some extreme cases, you might be liable for a lawsuit under clauses relating to "trade secrets."

So, you have remembered your professional and personal manners and you are leaving with your reputation intact, along with your employer's good wishes for your future. It's a wonderful, exciting time. There is an element of risk as you assume new responsibilities and have to learn to work with a different set of personalities within a different company culture. But life is moving on—and so are you! ■

14

What Kind of Training Is Needed?

One of the first questions we ask, when a young designer calls our office looking for a job, is what school he or she attended. It's not a question of whether the designer has a degree, but a question of where that degree was obtained. The content and quality of design education is significantly different from one institution to another. For us it may mean the difference between scheduling an immediate interview or asking the designer to drop off his or her portfolio. This is a clear indication of how significant the quality of education is for the designer in the job market.

General Characteristics of Design Education

Simply put, a common syllabus for graphic design education does not exist in the colleges of United States. Design is a creative process, and therefore, completely subjective. Design education is dependent upon the vision and insights of those who are responsible for hiring faculty and structuring curriculum and its content. Each institution teaches design from a somewhat different point of view. To confirm this, one only has to examine the portfolios of graduating students. The educational focus and graphic style of these portfolios are, in most instances, so distinctive, it is possible to identify the graduate's college just by looking at them. It is easy to understand how selecting a college could very well enhance or limit future career choices.

Since design programs are different, let us look at some of the primary paths and choices. Initially we need to acknowledge that almost every university has an art department; however, those departments' curricula focus on the traditional fine arts, such as drawing, painting, print making, and sculpture. Our analysis here is limited to "professional" programs—the education required to enter the graphic design field. Since the field is so competitive, it is necessary to value and evaluate the pressure put on graduates seeking their first job. We have acknowledged in previous chapters the importance of those first career steps, and how every advantage can help. The educational process is, naturally, the fundamental preparation for those first steps.

An Idiosyncratic Curriculum

As stated, design, unlike mathematics or physics, does not have a fixed set of standards to follow. Each school has its own conception of the meaning and function of design. For the unsophisticated, these are subtle distinctions and the distinguishing philosophical features of a curriculum which are only appreciated by professionals. Researching educational institutions may only compound the dilemma, for the jargon used in college or art school catalogues only confuses and emphasizes the fact that they are teaching vastly different majors—i.e., visual communications, graphic design, or media arts, to name a few. Programs with comparable fields of concentration in design are not offered by every institution with an art program. There is no uniformity in degrees offered either, so a Bachelor of Fine Arts (BFA), Bachelor of Arts (BA), or Bachelor of Science (BS) may be earned. Moreover, course requirements for the same degree will not necessarily be the same. Compounding the confusion, different programs even receive different accreditation. However, one key criteria should always be kept in mind. Design education is not the same as fine arts education. The nature of design is that it is a business, servicing the client and consumer, not a self-fulfilling creative exploration. Therefore, the curricula of a design program should be focused towards professional goals.

What distinguishes graphic design programs and how

does one become an educated consumer in choosing a school? Furthermore, what is the net result or goal of the educational focus? Perhaps, more directly, what do the best graduate portfolios look like, and is it possible to control what kind of careers the graduates achieve? One excellent way to answer these questions is to ask practicing professionals, especially if they are in a position to evaluate newly graduated and young designers. It is often particularly helpful to know what their own educational and work background has been. They can then possibly be in a position to recommend schools on the basis of their own experience and hiring practices. While their responses will probably be highly subjective, they will nonetheless give a direction.

Faculty: The Key Influence

The curriculum of any art institution is only as strong as the faculty, for in many instances there is no written curriculum, but merely a course outline. Therefore, the importance of the faculty input to the overall educational experience and achievement cannot be overemphasized. The teacher's own training and life experience will determine his or her aesthetic value system and may establish different levels of professionalism. The classroom situation rests on an ever-changing dynamic between students and instructors. Determining what is good, true, and right in art and design is a fundamental, recurring question whose answer is in constant flux.

It's common practice for most art schools located in major cities to hire instructors who are working professionals for their day-to-day experience and insights. These part-time faculty are individuals that may teach only one class or one day a week. They often teach a specialized subject and bring into the classroom projects from their current work environment. The "real world" atmosphere of these classes simulate, in many respects, a working atelier. Students may be recruited by faculty to work as apprentices in their studios. These experiences can be invaluable. Some institutions also actively and aggressively place their students into firms on co-operative work/study programs (co-ops) that offer actual work experience with college credit. The quality of these faculty/student relationships vary in direct correlation to the

Work/Study Programs

compatibility of their personalities. It is very hard to qualify the academic merit, but the pragmatic value becomes self-evident by the quality of the output. In gauging professional art schools, the term "professional" often refers to the number of design or advertising professionals on staff as visiting professors, compared to professional educators. Studying the listing of faculty and their accompanying bios can be more instructional than reading the class syllabus. It is these faculty members, and their points of view, formed by their life experience, that will formulate the course content.

Schools may also call upon a sizable pool of professional talent that is not available for long-term teaching commitments, but represents a valuable resource for guest lectures, expert critiques, and intensive workshops. Institutions outside the main city centers use various techniques, such as flying in critics and guest lecturers and organizing field trips for students, but must rely on an established, full-time faculty.

Frequent exposure to the diversified opinions of professionals, as well as their reinforcement of important, underlying truths, will better equip the student to make intelligent, necessary career choices. Competent teachers who have specialized in different areas of design can provide desirable role models. The position role models can play in formatting a direction of education should not be undervalued. The role-model process and the luxury of being exposed to superior talent in a formative period of life are some of the most enriching experiences any education can offer.

In Search of a Contemporary Curriculum

The importance of an academic curriculum should not be underestimated. The graphic designer is an arbiter of the times and must be aware of cultural and political currents. The designer, therefore, must have a well-rounded education in order to be sensitive to these issues. It is critical to choose an institution that offers a balanced curriculum. You may also opt for a graduate-level or an advanced certificate program in graphic design, which can offer the specialized focus for those who have come from a traditional fine arts/liberal arts education. While this educational direction certainly represents a longer academic road, the combination of curricula produces an educationally flexible, well-grounded individual. The more obvious function of post-graduate work is its attraction to graphic designers who have achieved an undergraduate degree in graphic design. The programs most often offer intensified study within a particular design philosophy or simply a return to aesthetic goals after some years of work. While these programs represent a professional enhancement and personal enrichment, they do not represent critical educational requirements in the marketplace.

A Sample of Choices

The American Institute of Graphic Arts publishes a directory of schools offering art programs. The directory includes some 800 institutions. The National Association of Schools for Art and Design in Reston, Virginia, lists close to 200 schools in an eighty-page directory. The sheer number of choices can be daunting.

The following is a short and highly subjective list of schools, compiled and based on observations during years of reviewing graduating student portfolios. It is a list of only those educational institutions I feel offer significant programs to prepare students to enter the graphic design field. Since the focus of graphic design education is crystallized in the graduates' portfolio, that resulting portfolio has become the hallmark of the educational success of the program, as well as the vehicle of entry to that first job. As faculty and program leadership change, so do the net effects (the relationship between faculty and syllabus having already been noted); thus this factor must become a consideration to any educational survey.

The wild card in any design education process is always the talent factor, for no matter what the quality of the education is, ultimately talent will out. Just as a mediocre student will not become a major talent no matter how superior the training, a great talent (with sufficient ambition) will overcome major obstacles. Individual creativity is such a strong factor in the finished product (the portfolio), that ultimately it becomes very clear, that this creativity has the power to surpass any educational dogma. The "individual" quotient in portfolios is also a major factor. Any person in a position to review many portfolios cannot help but observe, just as no two faces or no two fingerprints are alike, neither are two portfolios. For me, that is the mystery and beauty of the process.

How to Contact Colleges

To receive detailed information about a school's programs, admission, tuition, and scholarships, contact the admissions office. It is a good idea to ask the admissions office or the placement office about their data on graduates; where the majority find employment. Always check the faculty listings and read their biographies. Try to get a sense of the ratio between tenured and visiting faculty. Full-time faculty offer stability and vision to a program; however, sometimes it is the visiting faculty (i.e., working professionals who teach) that give a program its vitality and link to current issues. To get a more personal feel for the program's point of view, I would suggest contacting the department chairperson.

It should be noted that New York City, befitting its reputation as the Big Apple, has more graphic design programs than any other major metropolis. The unique quality of these programs, existing within the most concentrated work environment and the communications capital of the nation, provides these schools with a large teaching pool of design professionals. It is not unusual for a visiting professor to teach different courses at different schools. Most schools in New York and other metropolitan areas have extensive evening programs as well, which may offer specialized courses, degrees, or programs.

An Educational Short List

The following is an educational short list, divided into three classifications: Undergraduate Graphic Design and Advertising, Undergraduate Industrial Design, and Graduate Programs. The institutions with important industrial design programs are indicated by an asterisk (*). New York City regional schools are separated because of their unique interrelationship. There is a separate list for graduate programs. These are all institutions which hold significant enough status to be singled out. While these institutions do not guarantee success, they are at the forefront of design education. The bottom line is that the student attending a school of repute, who has the innate talent, curiosity, commitment, and passion for design, and is willing to work hard, will succeed. ■

Undergraduate Programs

Art Center College of Design*

1700 Lida Street
Pasadena, CA 91103
(818) 584-5000

Brigham Young University

Visual Communications Design
Provo, UT 84602
(801) 378-3890

California School of Arts and Crafts* (Cal Arts)

1700 17th Street
San Francisco, CA 94103
(415) 703-9500

Carnegie Mellon University

Design Department
110 Margaret Morrison
Pittsburgh, PA 15213
(412) 268-2828

Illinois Institute of Technology Institute of Design

Chicago, IL 60616
(312) 567-3250

Kansas City Art Institute*

4415 Warwick Boulevard
Kansas City, MO 64111
(816) 561-4852

Kent State University*

School of Art
Kent, OH 44242
(216) 672-2192

Portfolio Center of Atlanta

125 Bennett Street N.W.
Atlanta, GA 30309
(800) 255-3169

Portland School of Art

97 Spring Street
Portland, ME 04101
(207) 775-3052

Rhode Island School of Design*

2 College Street
Providence, RI 02903
(401) 331-3511

Rochester Institute of Technology*

Bausch & Lomb Center
1 Memorial Drive
Rochester, NY 14623
(716) 475-2411

Syracuse University	Department of Visual Communications
	102 Shaffer Art Building
	Syracuse, NY 13244
	(315) 443-4071
The University of the Arts*	Broad & Pine
	Philadelphia, PA 19102
	(215) 875-4800
University of Cincinnati*	2624 Clifton Avenue
	Cincinnati, OH 45221
	(513) 556-6000

New York City Region

The Cooper Union	41 Cooper Square
	New York, NY 10003
	(212) 353-4120
FIT (State University of New York)	227 West 27th Street
	New York, NY 10001-5992
	(212) 760-7673
Parsons School of Design	66 Fifth Avenue
	New York, NY 10011
	(212) 741-8900
Pratt Institute*	School of Art & Design
	Brooklyn, NY 11205
	(718) 636-3600
School of Visual Arts	209 East 23rd Street
	New York, NY 10010-3994
	(212) 679-7350
SUNY Purchase (State University of New York)	735 Anderson Hill Road
	Purchase, NY 10577
	(914) 251-6000

Graduate Programs

Art Center College of Design	Pasadena, CA
Basel School of Design	Basel, Switzerland
Cranbrook	Bloomfield Hills, MI
Pratt Institute	Brooklyn, NY
Rhode Island School of Design	Providence, RI
Santa Fe College of Design	Santa Fe, NM (opening September 1997)
Yale	New Haven, CT

15

Past, Present, and Future

In the introduction to this book I discussed why everyone should have the luxury of choice. I believe that the importance of recognizing life's choices and following one's intuition is key to realizing individual potential. Sometimes these choices offer surprising opportunities and directions never considered. It's always interesting to ask accomplished people, who seem to have a clear direction to their lives, what they thought they were going to be when they began their careers. There are many surprises awaiting in those answers. (Certainly no one grows up saying they want to become a "headhunter"!) In the early stages of a career there is a sense that all the important choices are being made at that time and that the die is permanently cast. Of course, it is a very formative period in one's life, but, having passed through this phase, I can assure you, your choices are not complete, and not over. It's no time to rest on past decisions and feel that the hard work is over. As you move into the mature periods of your career, know that the ability to make these transitions is a positive step. What a wonderful way to anticipate the future. It is a future full of choices, full of decisions, full of change—and therefore full of promise.

Change: The Only Constant

It is important to perceive your career as a creative challenge, as one to be molded and formed by many sequential choices. The challenge of a creative career is the ability to achieve continuous progress and advancement. You should always have the sense of growing. The new should be wonderful and exciting, and faced with some apprehension—but not fear. We all know people, and role models, who continue to be vital influences and achievers late into life. And we all know those who seem to be beaten down, tired, and lacking a sense of purpose. Sustaining your intellectual curiosity, energy level, passion, and optimism for work and life are critical goals for all to attain. This is how we remain fresh and enjoy the unique gift of creativity.

Fortunately or unfortunately, nothing is forever. We all function in a state of flux and things never stay the same. Technology, demographics, and economics constantly change the landscape of opportunity. Business, by definition, is in a state of continuous flux. Firms form, grow, and change structure. Perhaps companies downsize or perhaps new partnerships are formed. Clients change, move from company to company, sometimes country to country. Communications styles change, taste levels change—always moving in new directions.

Keeping up is, for most, the hardest chore. And some designers don't keep up. Relying on tried and true formulas, they unhappily learn their proven methods aren't so tried and true. Somehow they have fallen behind, grown stale—and, worse yet, dated. Creative "burnout" is a serious and dangerous problem in design and advertising. We work in a business environment that has an insatiable appetite for the new. The competition is keen (some would say brutal) and the work load very demanding. A continuous new crop of bright, young talent entering the scene every year can easily create a justified paranoia in the insecure. This problem becomes an occupational hazard for the person whose talent has not continued onto new plateaus. Unless designers who have lost their spark can move into senior positions with administrative or marketing/sales responsibility, they become the casualties of our creatively driven business, for they can get "tired" without the excitement and enthusiasm of the new.

The Future Belongs to . . .

Our graphic designer of the future is a fortunate person. This is an individual who will have wonderful resources to draw upon. It is an exciting time. The business is changing.

Graphic design has felt the same technological, demographic, and economic effects over the last ten years as every other segment of our society. The working structure within design firms has changed. Our technological age has released a revolution in the way we communicate and the manner in which we work. We have also witnessed the unanticipated and amazing demographic swing toward a work force with a female majority. Our designer of the future will function in a world compressed by technology, challenged by the new medias of the future, enhanced by new options for communication, and controlled, as always, by economics.

The 1980s witnessed a period of intense merger and acquisition activity. Many advertising agencies and design firms underwent the sometimes painful transitions of unification. Now that partnerships have aged and buy-out agreements have matured, a new structuring and a second generation of leadership is appearing. Some firms, disenchanted with the existing relationships, are buying themselves back. Firms are reconsidering their service offerings. Some are diversifying. Some are reinvestigating the process and methodology of their services. Some see a convergence of design and advertising. Integrated marketing is seen by some as the way to the future and technology will give direct marketing the ability to position and fine tune messages beyond anybody's dreams. The capability of the digital communications environment now and into the next century are constantly challenging our perceptions of how to define the future. The net effect is that new opportunities are always emerging. What an exciting time to be a witness and participant!

A global business order is a reality for most of the larger firms and rapidly evolving for some of the smaller. Global marketing is a driving force behind many products, services, and identity programs. The ability to understand foreign languages and customs is increasingly important. New markets in the Asian rim countries are expanding. After the Japanese commercial explosion, Thailand, Hong Kong, Taiwan, Indonesia, Singapore, and Korea have become important markets. The rush is on to expand markets in Vietnam and China. South America is currently perceived by financiers as the next major market for development. The European Eastern Bloc countries are reforming. They will have their own needs and centers for commerce.

The graphic designer will play his or her role all over the world. Adaptability and flexibility will be important personality traits. The graphic designer of the future will be required to have the necessary creative talent, to demonstrate the intellectual savvy for the "big picture," be able to grasp the marketing strategies, possess the knowledge to access the latest technology, and exhibit the sensitivity to work with different cultures. This individual will have to wear many hats, and assume many guises. The graphic designer will become a true renaissance personality.

So, always recognize the mark of the future. It is today! ■

Appendix

Professional Societies

In any discussion of graphic design groups it is helpful to
know which professional groups are associated with which
area of specialization. These organizations promote their
area of interest and offer their memberships a variety of
enriching programs. The following list represents some of the
better-known groups. It may be helpful to contact them for
information. Some have membership lists of firms that can be
useful when you want to search for a job in another city.
They may also be able to give you information about educational programs, seminars, newsletters, annual publications,
and exhibition programs. These organizations provide the
designer the forum to keep up and remain current, as
well as an opportunity to network and meet peers. The
groups marked with an asterisk (*) have regional chapters;
always check for those listings locally or with the national
organization.

American Center for Design (ACD)

213 West Institute Place, Suite 405
Chicago, IL 60611
phone: (312) 787-2018
fax: (312) 649-9518
e-mail: acdchicago@aol.com
www.ac4d.org

The American Institute of Graphic Arts (AIGA) *
(The AIGA has 35 local chapters.)

164 Fifth Avenue
New York, NY 10010
phone: (800) 548-1634 or (212) 807-1990
fax: (212) 807-1799
e-mail: AIGAnswers@aiga.com
www.aiga.org

Art Directors Club of New York *
(There are Art Directors Clubs in many cities,
most of which incorporate the name of the city,
or perhaps the state, i.e., The Art Directors Club
of New Jersey.)

250 Park Avenue South
New York, NY 10003
phone: (212) 674-0500
fax: (212) 228-0649
e-mail: adcny@interport.net
www.interport.net/adcny

The Design Management Institute (DMI)

29 Temple Place
Boston, MA 02111-1350
phone: (617) 338-6380
fax: (617) 338-6570
e-mail: dmistaff@dmi.org
www.dmi.org

Direct Marketing Association (DMA)

1120 Avenue of the Americas
New York, NY 10036
phone: (212) 768-7277
fax: (212) 302-6714
e-mail: dma@the-dma.org
www.the-dma.org

Graphic Artist's Guild *

11 West 20th Street, 8th Floor
New York, NY 10010
phone: (212) 463-7730
fax: (212) 463-8779
e-mail: paulAtGAG@aol.com
www.gag.org

Industrial Designers Society of America (IDSA) *

1142 Walker Road
Great Falls, VA 22066-1836
phone: (703) 759-0100
fax: (703) 759-7679
e-mail: idsa@aol.com

Package Design Council International (PDC) *

481 Carlisle Drive
Herndon, VA 20170-4830
phone: (800) 432-4085 or (703) 318-7225
fax: (703) 318-0310
e-mail: info@pkgmatters.com
www.packinfo-world.org

The Society of Environmental Designers (SEGD) *

401 F Street NW, Suite 333
Washington, DC 20001
phone: (202) 638-5555
fax: (202) 638-0891
e-mail: segdoffice@aol.com

Society of Illustrators

128 East 63rd Street
New York, NY 10021
phone: (212) 838-2560
fax: (212) 838-2561
www.members@aol.com/si39th

The Society of Publication Designers (SPD)

60 East 42nd Street, Suite 721
New York, NY 10165
phone: (212) 983-8585
fax: (212) 983-6043
e-mail: spdnyc@aol.com

Bibliography

AIGA Salary and Benefits Survey, 1994. New York: The
    American Institute of Graphic Arts, 1994.

The Art Directors Club. *The Art Directors Club Annual*. New
    York: The Art Directors Club of New York, annually.

Bayley, Stephen. *Taste*. London: The Conran Foundation,
    1983.

Chajet, Clive. *Image by Design From Corporate Vision to
    Business Reality*. Reading, MA: Addison-Wesley, 1991.

Crawford, Tad and Eva Doman Bruck. *Business and Legal
    Forms for Graphic Designers*. New York: Allworth
    Press, 1995.

Crawford, Tad. *Legal Guide for the Visual Artist*. New York:
    Allworth Press, 1995.

Graphic Design: USA. Published annually. New York: The
    American Institute of Graphic Arts.

Heller, Steven and Lita Talarico. *Design Career*. New York:
    Van Nostrand Reinhold, 1987.

Heller, Steven. *Graphic Design: New York*. New York: Rockport Allworth Editions, 1992.

International Design Conference in Aspen. *The New Business of Design*. New York: Allworth Press, 1996.

The Joint Ethics Committee. Code of Fair Practice. New York: The Joint Ethics Committee, 1989.

Laurel, Brenda, editor. *The Art of Human-Computer Interface Design*. Reading, MA: Addison-Wesley, 1991.

Leland, Caryn. *Licensing Art and Design*. New York: Allworth Press, 1995.

Mok, Clement. *Designing Business: Multiple Media, Multiple Disciplines*. San Jose, CA: Adobe Press, 1996.

National Association of Schools of Art and Design. *Directory 92*. Reston, VA: National Association of Schools of Art and Design, 1992.

Type Directors Club. *Typography*. New York: Type Directors Club, annually.

Vivid Studios. *Careers in Multimedia*. Emeryville, CA: Ziff-Davis Press, 1995.

Wurman, Richard and Peter Bradford, editors. *Information Architects*. Zurich: Graphis Press Corp., 1996.

PERIODICALS

American Center for Design. Publications and video presentations.

Communication Arts. Published eight times a year. Palo Alto, CA: Coyne & Blanchard.

The Design Management Institute. *The Design Management Journal* (quarterly series). Boston, MA: The Design Management Press.

Graphic Design: USA. Published monthly. New York: Kaye Publishing Corporation.

Graphis. Published bi-monthly. New York & Zurich: B. Martin Pedersen.

How. Published bi-monthly. Cincinnati, OH: F & W
   Publications.

The Journal of Business and Design. Boston, MA: Corporate
   Design Foundation.

Lippincott & Margulies. "No Image, No Premium." Chap. 5
   in *Identity and Image Management Issues*. New York:
   Lippincott & Margulies Inc..

Lippincott & Margulies. *Sense* (a periodical series). New
   York: Lippincott & Margulies Inc.

Multimedia Producer Magazine. Monthly. White Plains, NY:
   Montage Publishing.

Print. Published bi-monthly. Rockville, MD: RC Publications.

SEGD. *Messages*. Published quarterly. Cambridge, MA: The
   Society of Environmental Graphic Designers.

Step-By-Step Graphics. Published monthly. Peoria, IL: SBS
   Publishing.

Index

A

CAREERS BY DESIGN

H

headhunter, 114–115, 144, 167, 201
health, 57, 79, 107, 109, 117, 123, 145, 170–171
  testing, 160
history, 21, 26, 58, 70, 77, 78, 83, 90, 91. *See also* future.
Hoffman-LaRoche, 64
home, 14, 24, 124, 155, 171, 173, 182. *See also* family.
  furnishings, 72
  office, 88, 173–174
  products for, 76
Hypertext, 84, 96

I

IBM (International Business Machines), 22, 39, 52, 69, 143
IDCA, 9, 212
Identity and Centennial Graphics, 62–63
IDSA (Industrial Designers Society of America), 63, 166, 209
Illinois, Chicago, 9, 62, 130
illustration, 15, 54, 56, 58, 62, 71, 90, 94, 96, 152, 160, 209
image, 25, 35–36, 38, 40, 41, 43, 54, 69, 71–72, 77, 96, 106, 147, 169, 213
  consciousness of, 23
  corporate, 40, 72
  downloading, 84
  manipulation of, 90
  moving, 91. *See also* animation; broadcasting, television and radio; film; media.
  recognition of, 32, 38–39
  reduction of, 131
  retail, 41. *See also* design, retail; retail identity.
  self-, 31, 36, 153
  updated, 36–39, 42, 45
  visual, 23, 25, 32, 36, 37–38, 50, 51, 52, 53, 57, 90, 91, 92
imagination, 21, 71, 84, 88, 90, 132. *See also* creativity.
individuality, 14, 21, 26, 35, 44, 78, 85, 87, 89, 90, 91, 92, 98, 101, 122, 130, 141, 142, 143, 145, 147, 174, 194, 195–196, 201, 204. *See also* creativity and originality; talent.
  and reputation, 137
information, 54, 57, 58, 65, 69, 79, 92, 99, 111, 128, 145, 160, 204. *See also* design, information; design, informational.
  architecture of, 30, 50–53, 212
  dated, 83
  monetary, 166–167
  proprietary, 159, 189
  provider, 39
  systems, 50–53
  transfer, 87–88
  useful, 88
  vehicles, 40
innovation, 20, 35, 58, 76, 84, 85, 88, 93. *See also* creativity.
intellect, 25, 64, 92, 102, 147, 194, 202, 204
  right and left brain, 96, 100
Internal Revenue Service, 113, 123
Internet, 85, 96, 98. *See also* Web.
internship, 111, 193

intranet, 88
ISDA (Industrial Design Society of America), 80

J

Japan, 10, 20, 186
job, 13, 19, 33, 36, 37, 40, 45, 54, 57, 58, 62, 67, 69–70, 71, 79, 83, 87, 150. *See also* companies and employees; ethic, work; experience, work; opportunity, career; time, work; work load.
  and income, 21, 22, 24, 33, 45, 79, 87, 94, 97, 112, 114, 122, 125, 149, 158, 182, 188, 211
    and benefits, 158, 167–168, 170–174, 188. *See also* pension.
    from sales, 31
    performance-based, 123, 175
    salaried, 96, 110, 123, 149–151, 158, 161, 165–168, 174–178
    severance, 185–186
  and self-employment, 124–125, 155
  availability, 9
  changing, 13, 113, 122, 135–136, 142, 151, 166–167, 181–189
  description, 23, 30, 145, 146, 147, 148, 149, 154
  flexibility of, 148, 151
  freelance, 45, 59, 96, 97, 110, 123–125, 135, 157, 161, 173
  hiring, 9, 12, 55–56, 89, 90, 92–102, 110, 120, 121, 128, 134, 141–162, 168, 183, 185, 187, 188, 195
  interview, 97, 101, 106, 112–117, 128, 130, 131, 134, 143–144, 151–159, 165, 185, 191
    exit, 185, 187
  on "spec," 136, 137
  placement, 12
  promotion, 69–70, 146, 150, 158, 175, 181–182, 202
  references, 160–162, 183, 187
  rejecting offer of, 161–162
  replacement, 157, 183
  resignation, 12, 142, 155, 158, 182–186, 188–189
  search, 10, 105–115, 120, 123, 127, 141, 142, 144, 148, 151, 152, 166, 167, 192, 207
  security, 150
  sharing, 173–174
  staff, 9, 12, 44, 45, 56, 62, 95, 97, 123, 137, 142–143, 144, 185
    in-house, 79
    summer, 111
  titles, 142, 157
  turnover, 138, 151, 157
Joint Ethics Committee, Code of Fair Practice, The, 212

K

knowledge, 10–11, 12, 13, 26, 31, 91, 93, 95, 98, 128, 135, 145, 166, 204. *See also* worldliness.

L

Landor Associates, 39
language, 23, 39, 43, 85, 86, 91, 117, 130, 145, 151, 159, 184
  HTML. *See* Hypertext.

About the Author

Roz Goldfarb established Roz Goldfarb Associates, Inc. in 1985, a New York–based management consulting and recruitment firm specializing in design, new media, advertising personnel, management and consulting, and new business ventures, with prominent clients in every category of the global business world. Ms. Goldfarb's multidisciplinary skills evolved from many years of hands-on business management, her early training as a sculptor and painter, and her tenure as the director of Pratt Institute's Associate Degree Programs (The Pratt Phoenix School of Design) where she hired and trained numerous faculty as well as developed programs, design curricula, seminars, and foreign programs.

In addition to *Careers by Design,* Ms. Goldfarb is the author of *The Art of Consulting,* published in the *Design Management Journal,* Spring 1996. She is co-author of *The Cross-Cultural Corporation* with Henry Steiner and Ken Haas to be published in 1998 by Addison-Wesley. Ms. Goldfarb frequently addresses professional groups and has spoken at The International Design Conference in Aspen, The Art Directors Clubs of New York and Los Angeles, and the Art Directors and Artists Club of Sacramento about career opportunities and the changing design environment. She has also been a visiting guest lecturer and critic at Syracuse University, The School of Visual Arts, Art Center College of Design (as a Toyota Scholar), The Parsons School of Design, and Pratt Institute. Ms. Goldfarb established a scholarship in 1987 with the Art Directors Club of New York to further the education of talented design students who require scholarship aid. She is a member of the Board of Advisors of The Santa Fe College of Design, New Mexico, and The Advisory Council of Starting Over of New York, Inc.

Ms. Goldfarb holds a Master of Fine Arts degree from Pratt Institute and a Bachelor of Arts degree from Hunter College of the City University of New York, where she studied painting with Robert Motherwell.

Books from Allworth Press

The New Business of Design by the International Design Conference in Aspen (softcover, 6 × 9, 256 pages, $19.95)

Design Literacy: Understanding Graphic Design by Steven Heller and Karen Pomeroy (softcover, 6¾ × 10, 256 pages, $19.95)

Looking Closer: Critical Writings on Graphic Design
edited by Michael Bierut, William Drenttel, Steven Heller, DK Holland (softcover, 6¾ × 10, 256 pages, $18.95)

Looking Closer 2: Critical Writings on Graphic Design
edited by Michael Bierut, William Drenttel, Steven Heller, DK Holland (softcover, 6¾ × 10, 256 pages, $18.95)

Design Culture: An Anthology of Writing from the AIGA Journal of Graphic Design edited by Steven Heller and Marie Finamore (softcover, 6¾ × 10, 256 pages, $19.95)

Selling Graphic Design by Don Sparkman
(softcover, 6 × 9, 256 pages, $18.95)

Licensing Art & Design, Revised Edition
by Caryn R. Leland (softcover, 6 × 9, 128 pages, $16.95)

Business and Legal Forms for Graphic Designers, Revised Edition
by Tad Crawford (softcover, 8½ × 11, 208 pages, $22.95)

The Copyright Guide by Lee Wilson (softcover, 6 × 9, 192 pages, $18.95)

Legal Guide for the Visual Artist, Third Edition
by Tad Crawford (softcover, 8½ × 11, 256 pages, $19.95)

Electronic Design and Publishing: Business Practices, Second Edition
by Liane Sebastian (softcover, 6¾ × 10, 200 pages, $19.95)

The Business of Multimedia by Nina Schuyler
(softcover, 6 × 9, 240 pages, $19.95)

The Internet Publicity Guide by V. A. Shiva
(softcover, 6 × 9, 208 pages, $18.95)

Please write to request our free catalog. If you wish to order a book, send your check or money order to Allworth Press, 10 East 23rd Street, Suite 400, New York, NY 10010. Include $5 for shipping and handling for the first book ordered and $1 for each additional book. Ten dollars plus $1 for each additional book if ordering from Canada. New York State residents must add sales tax.

If you wish to see our catalog on the World Wide Web, you can find us at Millennium Production's Art and Technology Web site:
http://www.arts-online.com/allworth/home.html
or at **http://www.interport.net/~allworth**